Essential
Barcelona

by

GEORGE KEAN

George Kean is an experienced travel writer
who lives and works in Spain. He is the author
of three Spanish titles in the current series of
Essential guides.

AA

Produced by AA Publishing

REC COMTAL

PORTAL NOU

Donna Sant Pere

PASSEIG DE LLUIS COMPANYS

PASSEIG DE SANT

FIND + RENT A CAR.

AV. DE VILANOVA

RONDA SANT PERE

THROUGH PLAZA DE ALUMINADAND

ARC OF TRIOMF

WALK PAST SQUARE & down

STEEP in middle off.

JUSTICE PALACE

Written by George Kean
Peace and Quiet section
by Paul Sterry
Series Adviser: Ingrid Morgan
Series Controller: Nia Williams
Copy Editor: Antonia Hebbert

Edited, designed and produced by
AA Publishing. Maps ©
The Automobile Association 1992

Distributed in the United Kingdom
by the Publishing Division of The
Automobile Association, Fanum
House, Basingstoke, Hampshire,
RG21 2EA

The contents of this publication are
believed correct at the time of
printing. Nevertheless, the
publishers cannot accept
responsibility for errors or
omissions, nor for changes in details
given. We have tried to ensure
accuracy in this guide, but things do
change and we would be grateful if
readers could advise us of any
inaccuracies they may encounter.

A CIP catalogue record for this book
is available from the British Library.

ISBN 0 7495 0301 7

Published by The Automobile
Association

Typesetting: Microset Graphics Ltd,
Basingstoke
Colour separation: BTB Colour
Reproduction, Whitchurch,
Hampshire
Printed in Italy by Printers SRL,
Trento

*Front cover picture: Gaudí
architecture*

This book employs a
simple rating system to
help choose which
places to visit:

◆◆◆ do not miss

◆◆   see if you can

◆   worth seeing if
     you have time

INTRODUCTION

Barcelona is a must for the traveller in the 1990s. It is an ancient city, now going through a frenetic metamorphosis to be in the vanguard of urban communities in the 21st century. It is celebrating its past by renovating its old buildings, and, always innovative, it is introducing new architecture and extending the cultural participation of its people.

The amount of things to see and do in Barcelona is unusually generous for a city of its size. There is an immensely rich architectural legacy within its evocative medieval Gothic core. The same is true in the rest of the city, wherever Modernist architects raised buildings — challenging when new (late 19th-early 20th century) and delightful to see today. Some 40 museums and lots of art galleries satisfy different interests, and numerous cultural foundations are very active in the arts, as are the public authorities. The city has a strong tradition in music and theatre, and attracts the world's top performers. Add to that a mild climate, a varied and interesting cuisine, fine local wines and plenty of quality things to buy, including arts and crafts, antiques, high fashion and other designer items, and you get an idea of Barcelona. This is a city of great style — evident in shops, restaurants, bars, discos and on the street — and the nightlife is intoxicating.

Most of metropolitan Barcelona's four million

Montjuïc with its commanding view of the city has in the past allowed rulers to command the city's obedience

inhabitants celebrated the announcement in October 1986 that the city's fourth attempt to attract the summer Olympic Games had been successful. The XXV Olympiad in 1992 would be the justification for raising public and private funds to renovate the city, get rid of some severe urban problems and to build for the future. Under the direction of its charismatic mayor, Pasqual Maragall, the city was looking past the Olympics themselves for a continuing programme of change, to shape the city for the year 2000 and beyond. Twice before, Barcelona had used great events to regain confidence, improve and embellish itself and to attract world attention. The Universal Exhibitions of both 1888 and 1929 left legacies of grand buildings — but not much more, because the planning did not go beyond their closing dates. This time, the thinking has been more radical. The renovation inspired by the Olympics is giving the city a new face in many places, a better road system, enhanced sports and entertainment facilities, and, it is hoped, a new sense of integration for its less advantaged inhabitants, many of whose origins are elsewhere in Spain.

INTRODUCTION

All this is good news for visitors, although most will still find Barcelona bewitching for the old, intangible reasons. Barcelona somehow casts a spell, and repeated visits do nothing to lessen it – in fact the charm has increased since the mid-1980s, with Barcelona blossoming to become the Mediterranean's most scintillating centre of creativity. The other side to the city's extraordinary character is a tendency to introspection and self-satisfaction among its inhabitants. Outsiders are very rarely made to feel like insiders, and some Barcelonans give the impression of thinking that Barcelona is the centre of the universe. The reality is impressive enough however. The city is the buzzing nerve centre of a dynamic and industrious region – Barcelona is the capital of Catalunya, traditionally Spain's most culturally progressive and economically advanced region, and still at the forefront today. Reason enough, perhaps, for the Barcelonan's special sense of pride.

Tibidabo looks over the city and its suburbs to the Mediterranean

BACKGROUND

To understand Barcelona, you have to know
about Catalunya (otherwise known as Cataluña
or Catalonia). Catalunya, in the northeast of
Spain, is one of its 17 semi-autonomous regions
— still part of the Spanish state, but with a good
deal of independence. The regions have been
created in the progress to democracy within a
federal system since the death of the dictator
General Franco in 1975. Catalunya has around
15 per cent of Spain's population of 38 million
and 6 per cent of Spain's territory, but as the
country's most economically advanced region, it
produces around 20 per cent of Spain's gross
domestic product. Within its four provinces it
offers wide physical variety: high Pyrenean
peaks and lush valleys in Lleida and Girona
provinces; Lleida's bare and rugged
landscapes; one of the world's best known
holiday areas, the pine-backed coastline of the
Costa Brava (Girona province); the acclaimed
vineyards of Penedés and the serrated heights
of Montserrat mountain within Barcelona
province; and the wetlands of the Ebro delta in
Tarragona province. The city of Barcelona, now
a sprawling metropolitan area of over four
million people, is Catalunya's capital. Just under
two million live within Barcelona municipal area
itself. It is there that the Catalan parliament has
its seat and from where the *Generalitat*, the
executive branch, directs the region's affairs
under a statute from the central government in
Madrid, which many Catalans believe is still too
restrictive of their freedoms. The municipal
area of Barcelona is run by the *Ajuntament*. In
recent years, the Generalitat has been
controlled by a right of centre party with
nationalist aspirations, and the Ajuntament has
been run by the Catalan socialist party, with
different views about what is best for the city,
especially over matters related to the Olympic
Games. No visitor to Barcelona can for long
remain unaware of two personalities: the
president of the Generalitat, and the *alcalde*
(mayor) of Barcelona. The palaces which are
their seats of power face each other across
Plaça de Sant Jaume, where once there was a
Roman market place and, most likely, a good

Not seeing eye to eye: the palace of the Ajuntament (top) and Generalitat (bottom) face one another

deal of bartering went on, then as now. A very small nationalist movement calls for the complete independence of Catalunya from Spain. The main nationalist aspiration is for greater autonomy within the Spanish state. Catalans complain that they are more industrious than other Spaniards and that they fill coffers which Madrid empties wastefully in other parts of the country. They want greater freedom in foreign relations and, to the annoyance of Madrid, the president of the Generalitat makes many official visits abroad. He has also initiated an organisation for

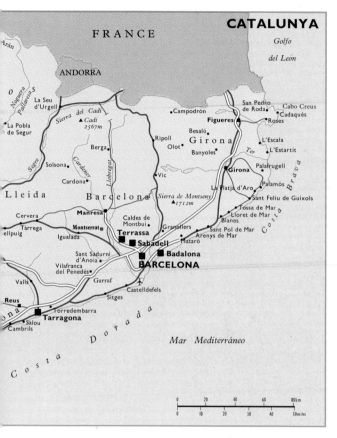

economic and political co-operation with other
regions in Europe and North America. Catalans
believe that, because of a different historical
experience, they have learned other, better
ways of doing things which it will be to their
advantage to apply in running the affairs of
their region. They also claim to have been a
nation centuries before there was a united
Spain: the Catalans are a people with a distinct
language and culture, found not only in the
present-day region of Catalunya, but also in the
regions of Valencia and the Balearic Islands, as
well as in Andorra and southern France.

BACKGROUND

The Catalan language developed from a version of Latin spoken in the northern regions of present-day Catalunya, and was widely spoken by the 9th century. Its great flowering as a written language happened in the 15th century. From the next century onwards it was rather obscured under the pressure of Castilian, which became the standard Spanish of today. In the early 1800s, however, during what is known as the *renaixença* or Catalan renaissance, there was a revival of interest in all things Catalan. The language flourished again over the following century, which culminated in 1932 with the publishing of the *Diccionari General*, the standard dictionary for the Catalan language. During the early years of Franco's rule it was forbidden to speak Catalan in public, but the language never died out. Today Catalan is an official language in Catalunya, ranking equally with Castilian Spanish. Catalan has also been officially recognised by the European Parliament, and was designated well beforehand as an official language of the XXV Olympiad. Its use is widespread in the media, business, cultural institutions and places of education.

Franco also threatened the Catalan language and culture in a more insidious way. From the 1950s he encouraged massive immigration to Catalunya from poorer regions of Spain such as Andalucia and Murcia, with the aim of watering down Catalan culture. Almost a million migrants arrived, mostly to work in and around Barcelona, where they lived in depressing, low-cost housing. Some did not find work, and neither have their children. Many have not integrated into Catalan society and it is unlikely that they will do so. It is widely said that the people from southern Spain are lazy, though nobody who has seen a construction worker or farmer working hard for very long hours in the hot sun can accept that proposition. However, they may be more willing to put off a job until tomorrow (*mañana*) whereas Catalans have a stricter work discipline and are generally eager to get on with a productive, well-rewarded career, whether it be in business or the arts. Catalans consider themselves to have the quality of *seny*, sound judgement, which makes them different from other Spaniards. Traditionally they have been more open to foreign influences and new trends than their compatriots, which has been to their advantage economically and culturally. This could be because of where they are on the European map, though some claim it is because of a cool and calculating temperament, more mid-European than Mediterranean. Elsewhere in Spain, it has been members of the landed aristocracy who have dominated society and been patrons of the arts. In Barcelona, it has been the mercantile class that has had most influence. The business community built fine mansions and sponsored the arts in the Middle Ages, and continues to do so. Cultural organisations founded by banks (*caixas*) are prominent, and business firms are paying for the restoration of long-neglected buildings, monuments and fountains around the city. Surprisingly in a city where business attitudes and influence are so strong, there is also an attitude that 'anything goes', and a freedom to be what you like. Creatively and morally Barcelona is a very open city — too much so for some visitors when they see what is sometimes presented as creative talent, or notice the hundreds of sex advertisements in the columns of quality newspapers. There is no doubt about the benefits to real creativity, however.

Fairytale Spain in the Poble Espanyol

Miró, Miró on the wall – and on the floor in the Fundació Miró

Artists working in Barcelona have gained great international acclaim. Among big names are Picasso, Miró, Casals, Rusinyol and Tàpies, principally painters; the architects include Gaudí and Sert; and among the musicians are Pau Casals, Montserrat Caballé and Josep Carreras. A few of the new names to be aware of are Miquel Barceló and Tomas Gomez, both painters; the sculptor Susana Solana; architects Bofill, Bohigas, Mackay, Martorell and Puig Domènech; designers Mariscal and Arribas; and the fashion designers Lola Barceló and Jose Tomas.

Visiting Barcelona

Guidebooks usually say the local people are friendly and welcoming. About Barcelonans it is more accurate to say they are correctly courteous to all visitors and that they are very welcoming to business people and people of artistic talent. Mr and Mrs Ordinary on a medium-cost vacation can expect fewer smiles than the industrialists, bankers and importers on business trips; and a city so much in the vanguard of contemporary culture gives a great welcome to any stars in the international arts galaxy. It also provides a friendly and encouraging environment for creative people who are talented but still unknown.

Barcelona has been best known as a city of trade and industry. Founded as a Roman trading and administrative post, it reached its zenith as leader among the Mediterranean's medieval port cities. In the 18th century, after centuries of obscurity, its textile industry again brought wealth and influence, and today it leads once more among port cities of the Mediterranean. It is a major industrial city and has growing significance as a financial centre. Curiously, neither the private nor public sectors has extensively exploited the tourism potential of Barcelona. It is as if the Barcelonans, who control Catalunya's purse strings, have thought that high-volume tourism was something which should only happen in the summer along Catalunya's coast — the Costa Brava, Costa Maresme and Costa Dorada. During weekdays it is difficult to find hotel accommodation in the city, as rooms are occupied by visitors to the city's many trade fairs and conferences. New hotels are being built, but too few to relieve the problem significantly. Tourist authorities have, by necessity, promoted the city as a weekend break destination. It is ideal for that, if you just want a taste, but Barcelona demands much more time to discover.

A solution to the accommodation problem is to stay during weekdays at one of the coastal resorts, from Blanes to Tarragona, which have a regular rail connection to Barcelona, and to make daily excursions to the city. Then stay in the city over the weekend and make the most of its exuberant nightlife.

Most tourists come in high summer when it is hot and humid. In spring and autumn the weather is more agreeable however, and people are not skulking in the shade but enjoying the streets, parks and outdoor cafés. Outdoor Barcelona can also be enjoyed on the many clear, but sometimes very crisp, winter days. The weather makes Barcelona an all-year destination, and the calendar of cultural events is full throughout the year. Despite that, a survey before 1992 showed that only 21 per cent of the city's visitors came for strictly tourist reasons — principal attractions were the Barri Gòtic, La Rambla and the Sagrada Família. Most of the visitors who came for trade fairs and congresses did not even visit any of these. Until recently, the main tourist attraction in this corner of Spain was the low cost of vacations on the coast. Spain generally is no longer the country for low-cost holidays however, and in Barcelona prices have risen well above the national average. The pattern of visitors is likely to change as the huge publicity of the Olympics spreads and informs more people internationally of the city's appeal. It may be that Barcelona becomes rather more known for its cultural and other attractions than as a city of trade and industry.

Barcelona has two problems common to most large cities. Tourists complain most about the city's pollution and street crime. A thick layer of polluted air often hangs, unmoving, above the city, and the streets are blocked with traffic four times a day as private cars, buses, taxis and goods vehicles noisily do battle for space. Civil action groups are trying to encourage the greater use of public transport while new roads are being built and faster traffic flow schemes introduced. The wider use of lead-free petrol and better emission controls on vehicles and factories will help but it is also likely that with increasing affluence there will be more and more cars coming on to Barcelona's roads. Then there are parts of the city, like either side of La Rambla towards the port, which visitors should quite simply avoid for their personal safety; other danger areas are some parts of metro and bus lines. Much of the street crime is committed to sustain a personal drug dependence, and there are drug rehabilitation schemes to combat the problem. The authorities are also smartening some of the most run down areas in the inner city where crime breeds, fed by deprivation. Visitors can play their part by taking the precautions sensible in any city.

The Making of Barcelona

Barcelona's present shape and appearance have evolved over many centuries. In prehistoric times, Iberian people lived in the hinterland of present-day Barcelona, and the Laietani tribe had a settlement in close proximity. Phoenician and Greek traders are known to have visited these shores, and the Carthaginians set up an encampment named Barcino after the general, Hamilcar Barca.

Roman Barcelona dates from the 2nd century BC and was centred on the low mound of Mont Taber, which is almost at the heart of the Barri Gòtic. It grew to be a trading and administrative town of some 30 acres (12 hectares) under the jurisdiction of the very much larger town of Tarraco (Tarragona). Parts remain of the town wall which dates from the late 3rd century, and excavations under the Plaça del Rei and the Museu d'Història de la Ciutat have revealed ruins of the Roman town. They also show traces of the sojourn of the Visigoths, who made Barcelona their capital in the Iberian peninsula for a brief period in the 6th century. There is no evidence that the Moors and Franks, who in turn controlled the town over the next centuries, prized it highly or expanded it. In the 870s counties of the Franks south of the Pyrenees became united under Count Wilfred the Hairy (878–97) and thereby the House of the Counts of Barcelona was founded. With the expansion of the court and religious institutions Barcelona began to experience real growth. By the 12th century, trade within the Mediterranean was already extensive and this grew faster during the reign of Ramon Berenguer IV (1131–62). Through the marriage of this count, Catalunya and the neighbouring kingdom of Aragón joined in a federation under a single crown but with each keeping its laws, language and customs. The

Roman foundations on display in the Museu d'Historia de la Ciutat

federation took Mallorca, Ibiza and Valencia from the Moors during the reign of Jaume I, The Conqueror (1213–76). Trade had another big boost and in Barcelona there was much building, including new town walls around an area some 10 times bigger than that enclosed by the previous walls. Mercenary admirals Roger de Lluria and Roger de Flor, who became great folk heroes, helped the count-kings of Barcelona and Aragón acquire Sicily, Athens, Corsica and Sardinia by 1324, when Barcelona was at the zenith of its power. Under Jaume II (1276–1327) more big building projects, including the great Gothic cathedral, were started. Pere IV (1336–87) was also a keen builder, one of whose projects was the beautiful Saló del Tinell.

In Catalunya the power of the count-king came under the scrutiny of the Corts, a parliament of three chambers made up of the nobility, clergy and mercantile class. The aristocracy and rich merchants were also active builders, commissioning their fine houses within what is today called the Barri Gòtic, and along streets like Carrer Montcada. All this went on while the Black Death, which broke out in 1348, and other plagues were decimating the population. In 1359, the Corts created the Generalitat, an executive of 24 members, to manage the country's budget. By the end of the 14th century, the Barri Gòtic, as we see it now, had largely taken its final shape, and Barcelona had been endowed with one of the world's most

The 19th century saw the city grow at breakneck speed

beautiful and evocative city districts. But the
city had by then also entered a period of
socio-political difficulties and eventual
economic decline.

The line of the House of Barcelona ended when
Martin I died without an heir in 1410, and
Catalunya became a partner in the crown of the
burgeoning central kingdom of Castile. It
retained its ancient rights, *constitucions*, by
which the monarch's powers were limited in
Catalunya. The Catalan civil war between 1462
and 1473 wrecked the economy and, although
there was some recovery, Catalunya was of less
interest to Castilian rulers looking west towards
the Americas after 1492. (Barcelona was
specifically excluded from trade with the
Americas.) During the War of the Spanish
Succession (1700–14), Catalunya, and especially
Barcelona, opposed the Bourbon claimant,
Felipe V, but he was eventually recognised as
king and punished the Catalans by revoking
their *constitucions*. Although there was much
bitterness, Barcelona's business community
initiated a slow recovery. Trade with the
Americas was again permitted, textile
industrialisation began and there was a big
growth in population. The Napoleonic Wars
(early 1800s) halted the forward movement, and
poverty and disease helped fuel the social
unrest which sparked sporadic outbursts of
mass violence through the 19th century. The
Barcelona business community, ever eager to
get on with profit making, saw to it that there
was economic progress in spite of the local
unrest and Spain's political chaos during this
time. Increasing profitability from more
mechanisation of the textile industry was the
main plank for the growing wealth of this group.
It supported the *renaixença*, an awakening of
interest and pride in all things Catalan from
poetry to architecture.

By the mid-19th century, the very rapidly
growing population made extension of the city
essential, and a competition was arranged to
find the best urban plan. Ildefons Cerdà won
the competition of 1859 with his very
formalised, modern scheme for the *Eixample*
('Extension' in Catalan), and work began 10
years later. Meanwhile civic and business

confidence was booming, and Barcelona decided to show itself off to the world. The Universal Exhibition of 1888 attracted over two million visitors to its site based around the Parc de la Ciutadella. Montjuïc hill was the main site for Barcelona's next Universal Exhibition in 1929. In the intervening 41 years the city had seen a doubling of the population, unplanned growth, strikes, anarchy and terrorism of which the most remembered outbreak is the *Setmana Tràgica* (Tragic Week) of 1909, when some 70 religious buildings were destroyed. There had also been the coming and going of the *Modernista* (Modernist) architects and craftspeople. They created for the city an architectural heritage which, together with its Gothic inheritance and much of what is being raised today, gives Barcelona a just claim to be among the world's richest cities architecturally.

Modernism

In the latter part of the 19th century artistic trends in several countries developed into what can conveniently be grouped together as Art Nouveau. The trend in Catalunya was called Modernism and it showed important distinctions from the others: it had strong nationalist overtones, and became the fullest expression of the Catalan *renaixença*. It was widely adopted with enthusiasm by the wealthy Barcelonans. The visitor's first encounter with Modernism (and he or she cannot easily escape it) will probably be the façades of the many mansion blocks, mainly in the Eixample, which were designed for the wealthy by architects such as Antoni Gaudí, Domènech i Montaner, Puig i Cadalfach, Josep Vilaseca and others. Modernism also found expression in the crafts used to decorate the buildings: those of the sculptor, ceramicist, glazier, ironworker, woodworker and cabinetmaker. But it also influenced painting, sculpture, graphic art, literature, bookbinding and even the way people dressed and conducted their lives. In one of those anomalies of Barcelona, a revolutionary artistic trend became almost the philosophy of its most conservative group. There were always some who detested Modernism — for them it was tasteless and excessive — but the general enthusiasm for it lasted until the 1920s (the new trend then was *noucentisme*, a return to classical inspiration which was shared with much of Europe).

The dominant style inspiration for Modernist architects was Catalan Gothic, which permitted them to celebrate the architectural achievements of Catalunya's golden age. To this they added more or less what they liked — usually extensive decoration, using varying combinations of crafts. Domènech i Montaner's Palau de la Música Catalana is one of the best examples of the use of mixed decoration. What might at first seem to be the most unacceptable juxtaposition of subjects, styles and materials comes together in a whole of great harmony and beauty.

The master of Modernism however was Antoni Gaudí. He graduated in 1878 and his earliest architectural work showed the influence of Catalan Gothic. In buildings such as the Casa Vicens and Palau Güell, both completed in 1888, he added elements of the Mudéjar style

The attraction of Gaudí's work is not just its dramatic scale but also the superb detail, as here in the Parc Güell

developed by medieval Moorish craftsmen in Spain. But he was soon following a singular path in which the principal inspiration for form was nature itself — its flowing lines and organic shapes. This posed many technical difficulties for which he found audacious solutions. Gaudí's work is also distinguished by the uniquely creative ornamentation of his buildings, both outside and inside. He worked closely with some of the leading craftspeople to furnish the architectural spaces he created with wrought iron, stained glass, sculpture and mosaics as well as furniture itself. The Güells, a family of rich industrialists, were Gaudí's main patrons, giving him many commissions and introductions. A religious zeal which found release in his work on the Sagrada Família cathedral overwhelmed his later years. In 1926 he died in a Barcelona hospital, unrecognised because of his scruffiness. The city's most famous architect had been run over by a tram.

Infighting between anarchists and socialists undermined the Republican cause

Dark Years

Spain's king, Alfonso XIII, fled the country in 1931 when it was clear from municipal elections that the electorate wanted a republic. Francesc Macià, previously exiled, became president of the Generalitat. Spain declared the Second Republic, but by the end of 1935, 28 governments in Madrid, of varying complexions, had been unable to stabilise the chaos in the nation. The Popular Front, an alliance of the Left, gained power after elections in February 1936, but chaos continued. In July, army factions, so-called Nationalists, led by General Franco, rose against the government. The ensuing Civil War was horrific. The Republican government was based in Barcelona from May 1937 until the city was taken by the Nationalists in January 1939. It was a period of anarchy and faction rivalry but also of heroism and fortitude.

Barcelona shared in Spain's post-war privations but it was the first city to show recovery. Again the business community was demonstrating its *seny* by working to its own advantage within a new order. Although public manifestations of Catalanism were forbidden, clandestine support of their separate language and culture gave Barcelonans the spirit to rise above the dullness of Franco's oppressive centralism. During the dark years it remained more in touch with the outside world, and retained a vitality not found elsewhere in Spain. From the 1950s there was strong economic progress, as well as the massive immigration and ugly, unplanned growth which created many of today's urban problems.

Orientation

The city spreads across a flat area of some 12 square miles (20 sq km) between the Mediterranean on the east and a semicircle of hills running from the southeast to the northwest. It is divided into municipal districts which in turn are divided into *barris*. Montjuïc hill rises to 570 feet (173m) and a vantage point towards its seaward side is a good place from which to get a panorama of the city's principal areas of interest. Montjuïc itself is certainly one of those. Looking northeast along the coast are the old harbour, the 18th-century suburban development of Barceloneta, and the barri of Poblenou, where development of the Olympic Village has created a new residential zone. Looking inland, directly below Montjuïc is the barri of Poble Sec, and beyond the broad Avinguda del Paral-lel is the district of Ciutat Vella (Old Town) with its barris of Raval, Casc Antic and Sant Pere-Ribera, separated from each other by the northwest to southeast arteries of La Rambla (not to be missed) and Via Laietana respectively. La Rambla (or Las Ramblas) is a series of five streets forming one long avenue through the city. At its foot, Columbus stands atop his tall pedestal pointing in the wrong direction for America, which often confuses visitors. At the core of the Casc Antic (Old Quarter), there is the beautiful, medieval Barri Gòtic. Principal tourist attractions within Sant Pere-Ribera are the Carrer Montcada and Parc de la Ciutadella.

Plaça de Catalunya, communications hub of the city, lies at the upper end of La Rambla. North and west of it stretches the extensive regular pattern of the Eixample district, which is dissected by three grand avenues: Gran Via de les Corts Catalanes (northeast to southwest); Passeig de Gràcia (northwest to southeast); and Avinguda Diagonal (west to east). The barris of Dreta de l'Eixample and Sagrada Família are the most interesting within the Eixample.

Beyond Avinguda Diagonal and stretching into the lower reaches of the Collserola hills are the residential districts of Horta Guinardo, Gràcia and Sarria Sant Gervasi. The district of Les Corts lies at the southern end of Avinguda Diagonal and includes the barris of Pedralbés and Les Corts. Tibidabo, 1,740 feet (532m), is the highest point of the Collserola hills.

Suburbs of low-cost housing and industrial zones stretch north and south of the central city. Beyond lie the attractions of the beach resorts of Barcelona province: to the north, the Costa Maresme with resorts like Arenys de Mar and Mataró; to the south, the Costa Dorada with resorts like Castelldefels and Sitges. The airport is seven and a half miles (12km) south of the city and is served by both rail and bus connections.

Once a riverbed, the tree-lined La Rambla runs down to the sea

1992 and Beyond

The year 1992 was earmarked well beforehand as one of special significance in Spain, as the 500th anniversary of Cristobal Colom's (Christopher Columbus) first voyage of discovery, the year of EXPO'92 in Sevilla (the biggest-ever Universal Exhibition), Madrid's designation as European City of Culture and the Olympic Games in Barcelona from 25 July to 9 August. The people of Barcelona resigned themselves early on to the disruption and inconvenience of preparation for the Olympics, as a price for enhancement of the city, including solutions to some urgent urban problems. Had it all just been for a 16-day world media event, they would surely have rioted. They were bemused, sometimes amused, by the attendant political power-playing and the delays caused by political differences. The municipal elections of May 1991 were dubbed the 'Olympic Elections' as their prime prize was the prestige of being *alcalde* (mayor) at the time when the world's TV cameras were focused on the city. At first, Barcelona municipality believed that it could use private and business finance to prepare for the Olympics alone, and thereby claim that they were truly Barcelona's Games. Eventually however a consortium called COOB'92 was formed in March 1987, to prepare for and

organise the XXV Olympiad, involving
Barcelona City Council, the Generalitat of
Catalunya, the Spanish Government and the
Spanish Olympic Committee.

The scale of work for 1992 and beyond beggars
belief. By January 1991, cost estimates were
running at three times higher than the original
forecasts. Important projects intended for
completion by the start of the Games were
abandoned or postponed. But whatever
mistakes and miscalculations there may have
been, it is undeniable that, to achieve their
Barcelona 2000 Strategic Plan, Barcelona's civic
authorities have successfully garnered the
support of private enterprise, as well as that of
regional and central governments. The aim was
to provide the Games with excellent amenities
and to enhance the city for its people and its
visitors.

There are four Olympic Areas within the city
which come within a circle with a radius of just
over three miles (5km). Montjuïc has the main
Olympic Ring of installations. The Estadi
Olímpic was first built for the 1929 Universal
Exhibition, and has been restyled and rebuilt to
have a capacity for 60,000 spectators. The Palau
d'Esports Sant Jordi, with a capacity of 17,000 in
its main hall, is a spectacular new building by
architect Arata Isozaki; the Complex Esportiu
Bernat Picornell includes swimming and diving
pools with a spectator capacity of 5,000. Other
areas serve the sports of athletics, hockey,
baseball and rugby. The Institut Nacional de
Educació Física is a sports university catering
for 1,000 students, and is housed in a new
building by Ricardo Bofill. In the creation of the
Parc de Mar, Barcelona has found an easy
residential extension northwards, which has
also opened the city to its sea. Disused
industrial zones and two and a half miles (4km)
of beach were selected for the Olympic
Village, designed by Oriol Bohigas and
partners. Its 2,000 apartments are the
accommodation base for a middle class suburb,
Nova Icària, with good services, sports
facilities, a marina, conference centre, shops
and offices. Two tower blocks here rise to 436
feet (136m), and are Barcelona's tallest
buildings. The luxury Hotel de las Artes

occupies one of them. Vall d'Hebrón, in the working class district of Horta Guinardo, was designated the third of the Olympic Areas, with the Velodrome cycle track and the Press Village — another source of post-Olympics housing. Local people have also gained a new sports pavilion and improved facilities for tennis, football, rugby, hockey and swimming. Fourth of the Olympic areas is Diagonal on the municipal boundaries of Barcelona (Les Corts district), Esplugues de Llobregat and L'Hospitalet de Llobregat.The Diagonal area has seen the lowest level of investment as it already had very good sports facilities: Camp Nou (the stadium of FC Barcelona), the university's sports grounds, the Mini Estadi, Reial Club de Tenis Turó and Palau Blau Grana.

Two ring roads, the Cinturó del Litoral on the seaward side, and the Cinturó II in the shadow of the Collserola hills, have been the major components in the big scheme to solve the city's acute traffic congestion problems. The objective has been to make it possible to cross Barcelona in 15 minutes at a speed of 50 miles per hour (80km) between the motorways to the north and those to the south. The ring roads are complemented by improvements to link roads crossing the city, with new traffic control methods. The pedestrian has not been forgotten: central walkways including gardens

Not just a cycle track, the Velodrome is part of the city's Olympic vision

have been incorporated in roads like Aragó-Guipúscoa, Ronda del Mig and Carrer Prim.

Remodelling of the Estació del Nord has for the first time given Barcelona a central bus station for all long-distance services within the peninsula and abroad. The França railway station (Estació Barcelona Terme-França) has undergone considerable improvement, with development in the surrounding area for an exhibition hall, hotel and gardens. There have been extensions to metro lines, improvements to stations and the provision of new rolling stock. The redevelopment of the old port includes an international trade centre and a marina, plus commercial, cultural, recreational and sports facilities. It is also another opening of the city to its sea, which is a novelty for Barcelonans. The British architect Norman Foster designed the elegant Torre de Telecommunicaciones, rising to 853 feet (260m) on Tibidabo, to replace the many telecommunications installations which previously defaced the hill.

On the site of old railyards adjoining the Estació del Nord two grand cultural buildings have arisen. The Teatre Nacional has been designed by Ricardo Bofill, with a winter garden vestibule, library, exhibition hall and two auditoria (1,000 and 500 capacities) below its metal and glass roof. The Auditori has been designed by Rafael Moneo around a central patio crowned by a semi-open cupola, to provide a fully integrated centre for the performance, practice and study of music. In the barri of Laval, the Museu d'Àrt Contemporani, designed by Richard Meier & Partners, forms part of the redevelopment of the Casa de la Caritat convent into a centre of contemporary culture.

Along with all this new building goes the redevelopment of dilapidated areas like the old red light zone of Barri Xines, and the *nou urbanisme* programme of embellishing urban spaces with outstanding design and art. Some may mourn the passing of a certain colourful sleaziness, but Barcelona is approaching the year 2000 with all the zest and style that makes it one of Europe's most exciting cities.

WHAT TO SEE

There is a lot to see, and you will have to pace yourself to avoid physical and mental exhaustion. An overload of culture and nightlife is a real danger in this city. Allow time for just strolling and looking at the buildings — Barcelona's architecture is something to be savoured, so this book includes entries on the most interesting city districts as well as places to visit within them. Allow time for shopping and window shopping too.

Start your planning by getting a map. The one given free by municipal tourist offices is adequate, but you can buy more comprehensive maps at kiosks or bookshops.

Museums and Cultural Centres

Even if your interest in the subject matter of Barcelona's museums is not enough to motivate a visit, you may want to see many of them because of their buildings. Except for the Museu Etnològic and the Fundaciò Miró, they are housed in buildings which have been converted for the purpose and are often interesting in their own right. The Museu Picasso may be at the top of your itinerary anyway, but even those who have an aversion to the artist's work should try to see it — the museum occupies two Gothic palaces. Opposite on

Barcelona's dreaming spires

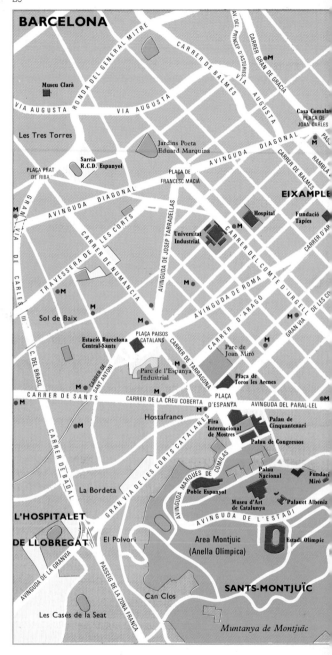

BARCELONA

Museu Clarà

Les Tres Torres

VIA AUGUSTA

VIA AUGUSTA

RONDA DEL GENERAL MITRE

CARRER DE BALMES

AV. DEL PRINCEP D'ASTURIES

CARRER GRAN DE GRACIA

VIA AUGUSTA

CARRER DE BALMES

Casa Comalat
PLAÇA DE
JOAN CARLES

Jardins Poeta
Eduard Marquina

Sarrià
R.C.D. Espanyol

PLAÇA PRAT
DE RIBA

PLAÇA DE
FRANCESC MACIA

AVINGUDA DIAGONAL

CARRER DE BALMES

RAMBLA

EIXAMPLE

AVINGUDA DIAGONAL

GRAN VIA DE CARLES

CARRER DE LES CORTS

TRAVESSERA DE LES CORTS

CARRER DE NUMANCIA

AVINGUDA DE JOSEP TARRADELLAS

Universitat
Industrial

Hospital

Fundació
Tàpies

CARRER D'AR

CARRER DEL COMTE D'URGELL

CARRER DE LES CO

GRAN VIA

Sol de Baix

AVINGUDA DE ROMA

AVINGUDA D'ARAGO

C. DEL BRASIL

Estació Barcelona
Central-Sants

PLAÇA PAISOS
CATALANS

CARRER DE
SANT ANTONI

Parc de l'Espanya
Industrial

CARRER DE TARRAGONA

CARRER D'ARAGO

Parc de
Joan Miró

Plaça de
Toros les Arenes

PLAÇA
D'ESPANYA

AVINGUDA DEL PARAL·LEL

CARRER DE SANTS

CARRER DE LA CREU COBERTA

Hostafrancs

Fira
Internacional
de Mostres

Palau de
Cinquantenari

Palau de Congressos

CARRER DE BADAL

La Bordeta

GRAN VIA DE LES CORTS CATALANES

AVINGUDA MARQUES DE COMILLAS

Poble Espanyol

Palau
Nacional

Fundació
Miró

Museu d'Art
de Catalunya

Palauet Albeniz

AVINGUDA DE L'ESTADI

L'HOSPITALET

DE LLOBREGAT

El Polvori

Area Montjuic
(Anella Olímpica)

Estadi Olímpic

SANTS-MONTJUÏC

AVINGUDA DE LA GRANVIA

PASSEIG DE LA ZONA FRANCA

Can Clos

Les Cases de la Seat

Muntanya de Montjuïc

Avinguda de Gaudí
C. DE MARINA
La Carrer Cenia
PLAÇA DE LES GLORIES CATALANES
Sagrada Família
CARRER D'ARAGO
CARRER DE BADAJOZ
Plaça de Toros Monumental
PASSEIG DE SANT JOAN
AVINGUDA DIAGONAL
Casa Macaya
CARRER D'AVILA
Casa Terrades
AVINGUDA
CARRER D'ARAGO
Museu de la Música
Mercat Concepció
PASSEIG DE LES CORTS CATALANES
PASSEIG DE
AVINGUDA DE LA MERIDIANA
asa Mila
Casa Montaner
Església de la Concepció
GRAN VIA DE LES CORTS CATALANES
GRAN VIA DE SANT JOAN
AVINGUDA DE CARLES I
DE GRACIA
Centre Permanent d'Artesania
Casa Batlló
Casa Amatller
Casa Leó-Morera
RONDA DE SANT PERE
CATALUNYA
Sant Pere
Palau de la Música
Parc de la Ciutadella
Museu d'Art Modern
Area Parc de Mar (Vila Olímpica)
niversitat
RONDA UNIVERSITAT
PLAÇA DE CATALUNYA
VIA LAIETANA
Palau de la Música
Museu de Zoologia
CATALANES
CARRER DE PELAI
CIUTAT VELLA
Museu de Geologia
Catedral
Museu Picasso
Estació Terme-França
Església de Betlem
Palau de la Generalitat
Museu d'Història de la Ciutat
Santa Maria del Mar
Hospital
Palau de la Virreina
Ajuntament
AVINGUDA D'ICARIA
CAVA BAR
RONDA DE SANT ANTONI
RAMBLA
× RISTORANT BAR
PLAÇA REIAL
La Barceloneta
Antic Hospital de la Santa Creu
PASSEIG DE COLOM
Moll de la Fusta
Gran Teatre del Liceu
DISCO QUEEN
Moll d'Espanya
Moll del Dipòsit
Platja de la Barceloneta
Museu de Cera
RONDA DE SANT PAU
Museu Marítim
AVINGUDA DEL PARAL·LEL
Poble Sec
Moll de Barcelona
Aeri
Acuario
PASSEIG DE JOSEP CARNER
Transbordador
Estació Marítima
AVINGUDA DE MIRAMAR
CARRETERA DE MIRAMAR
Castell de Montjuïc
Moll de Ponent
Moll del Levante
CINTURÓ DEL LITORAL
Moll de Contradique

0   300   600 metres

Carrer Montcada, another fine Gothic palace houses the Museu Tèxtil i de la Indumentària — worth a visit even if you have little interest in textiles and clothing. You need not be very keen on things maritime to appreciate the Gothic grandeur of the Museu Marítim; by way of contrast, a Modernist mansion, the Casa Quadras, is home to the Museu de la Música. The same goes for cultural centres: that of the Caixa de Pensions in Passeig Sant Joan is Casa Macaya, another building by the Modernist Puig i Cadalfach. Most museums are closed on Mondays. Entrance fees vary but none is very high. The main museums are described here, but there are many others, on subjects from geology to shoemaking.

Urban Spaces

Visitors to Barcelona have something new to appreciate as they move around the city: a bold attempt to make contemporary art part of the scenery. This is of greater significance in Barcelona than in most cities: within its *nou urbanisme* scheme, Barcelona is both creating urban spaces (*espais urbans*), or remodelling existing ones, which are being endowed with sculptures and design by leading contemporary artists. *Nou urbanisme* includes strict control on the quality of design and construction of new buildings. The Australian-born writer on architecture, Robert Hughes, an admirer of Barcelona, has described it as 'the most ambitious project of its kind undertaken by the Town Hall of any city in the 20th century', and in his recent memoirs, the architect Ricardo Bofill has written, 'We architects of Barcelona have learned anew how to make a city.'

A selection of urban spaces and architectural features is included in the entries which follow. *Parc* means park; *plaça* means square or plaza. If time is very short and you want to get some idea of the city's *nou urbanisme*, three very different examples of what is being done can be seen in the vicinity of Estaciò Sants: Plaça Països Catalans, Parc de l'Espanya Industrial and Parc de Joan Miró. But keep aware as you move around the city, and everywhere you will find evidence of this weaving of art into Barcelona's fabric.

Bus Turìstic (Bus 100)

From 23 June to mid-September, between 09.00 and 19.30 hours the Bus Turìstic (Bus 100) makes a circuit with 15 stops convenient for the main places of interest. A ticket valid for one day, or a half day from 14.00 hrs, allows unrestricted use and unlimited travel on five means of transport: Bus 100, Telefèric de Montjuïc, Funicular de Montjuïc, Tramvia Blau and Funicular del Tibidabo. More information and a route map can be obtained from tourist offices and TMB kiosks such as the one below Plaça de Catalunya. In the descriptions of places which follow, the stop number of Bus 100 is given in brackets. Remember it runs only for a limited period in the year.

◆◆◆
ANELLA OLÍMPICA
Montjuïc

The Olympic Ring spreads over the western crest of Montjuïc hill. The stadium built for the Universal Exhibition of 1929, with the Olympics of 1936 in mind, was gutted except for the façade, and the new **Estadi Olímpic** was designed by architects Gregotti, Milà, Correa, Buxadè, and Margarit. Gargallo's sculpture of the chariot racer, *Els Aurugues*, and the monumental marathon entrance gate have been retained. The old stadium site required excavating 36 feet (11m) to increase the seating capacity to 60,000 (originally intended to be 70,000 but reduced for safety reasons). Japanese architect Arata Isozaki coupled traditional architectural principles with modern technology and materials in his design of the **Palau d'Esports Sant Jordi**. For instance, the huge cupola is supported in the same way as the cupola on the cathedral of Florence and requires no interior pillars, which would restrict views in the arena. It can seat 17,000 spectators and has a six-lane athletics track with a perimeter of 200 metres. The cupola allows in daylight to save on lighting costs and also has acoustic panels, because the Palau Sant Jordi is a venue for concerts. It is the single most impressive, and expensive, building which has been raised for the Olympic Games, and for Barcelonans it is likely to remain the lasting symbol of 1992.

Sculptures in the adjoining plaça are by Aiko Miyawaku. The other sports complex within the Anella Olímpica, the **Complex Esportiu Bernat Picornell**, has two pools used for swimming, waterpolo and synchronised swimming. There is a new baseball field with stands for 1,000 spectators.

Olympic Stadium – great team work

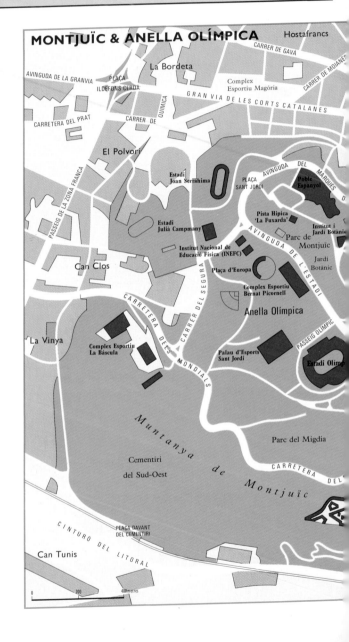

MONTJUÏC & ANELLA OLÍMPICA

Hostafrancs

CARRER DE GAVA

La Bordeta

Complex
Esportiu Magória

AVINGUDA DE LA GRANVIA

PLAÇA
ILDEFONS CERDÀ

CARRER DE MOIANÈS

GRAN VIA DE LES CORTS CATALANES

QUÍMICA

CARRER DE

CARRETERA DEL PRAT

El Polvorí

Estadí
Joan Serrahima

PLAÇA
SANT JORDI

AVINGUDA DEL

MARQUÈS

Poble
Espanyol

D

PASSEIG DE LA ZONA FRANCA

Estadi
Julià Campmany

Pista Hípica
'La Fuxarda'

Institut i
Jardí Botànic

Institut Nacional de
Educació Física (INEFC)

AVINGUDA DE L'ESTADI

Parc de
Montjuïc

Jardí
Botànic

Can Clos

Plaça d'Europa

Complex Esportiu
Bernat Picornell

Anella Olímpica

CARRER DEL SEGURA

CARRETERA DE'S

PASSEIG OLÍMPIC

La Vinya

Complex Esportiu
La Bàscula

Palau d'Esports
Sant Jordi

Estadi Olímp

MONDIALS

Muntanya

Parc del Migdia

Cementiri
del Sud-Oest

de

Montjuïc

CARRETERA

DEL

CINTURO DEL LITORAL

PLAÇA DAVANT
DEL CEMENTIRI

Can Tunis

0   200   400 metres

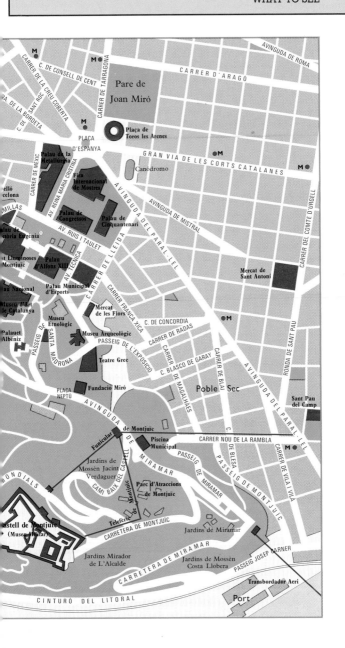

WHAT TO SEE

Ricardo Bofill had a Greco-Roman inspiration for his design of the Generalitat's **Institut Nacional de Educació Fisica** (INEF). This sports university has facilities for 1,000 students and 100 teachers and is arranged around two cloisters. Joining them is a vestibule and a hall for exhibitions and performances with a capacity of 2,000. Architects Canosa and Ferrater have been responsible for linking the various installations with three plaças, united by stairs and a cascade of water — this runs from the Estadi to the Plaça Europa, which has been built upon one of Europe's biggest water tanks. The *depósito* has a capacity of 78,000 cubic yards (60,000 cu m) to augment the city's supply. Redevelopment of Montjuïc is completed by the **Parc del Migdia** which slopes down the once-desolate south side of the hill next to the Cementeri.

The exhibitionist Arc del Triomf

Architect Galí and landscape designer Beth Figueres have been responsible for designing the 128-acre (52ha) site, in a scheme including 20,000 trees, the Jardí Botànic (botanic garden) and, on the site of a quarry, an open-air auditorium with a capacity of 100,000. This park is a striking example of how the Olympic Games have given the motivation and the means for improving the city. *Bus*: 61 from Plaça d'Espanya; 100 (stop 11).

◆◆
ANTIC HOSPITAL DE LA SANTA CREU
between Carrer de l'Hospital and Carrer del Carme, off La Rambla
This institution was first established in the 11th century as a hospice for ailing pilgrims. It makes a handsome assembly of Gothic buildings, now used by Catalan educational and cultural organisations. You can visit its peaceful courtyards and

view the buildings from the outside. The chapel is used for exhibitions: tourist offices and the local press should have details of what is on.
Metro: Liceu. *Bus*: 100 (stops 1 and 13).

♦
ARC DEL TRIOMF
Passeig de Lluis Companys
The arch symbolises the 1888 Universal Exhibition, to which it was the main entrance. With sponsorship from the department store chain El Corte Inglés, it has been restored to its former glory at a cost of 120 million pesetas.
Metro: Arc del Triomf.

♦
AVINGUDA DE GAUDÍ
Avinguda de Gaudí is a broad avenue joining two of the city's architectural sights: Gaudí's Sagrada Família and Domènech i Montaner's lesser-known Hospital de la Santa Creu i Sant Pau. As part of the *nou urbanisme* programme, the avenue has been redesigned by M Quintana to have a central walkway decorated with antique streetlamps and sculptures by Apel-les Fenosa.

♦
CAROUSEL DE LA GUARDA URBANA
La Fuxarda Pista Hípica, Parc de Montjuïc
The Carousel is a 40-minute display of horsemanship by the mounted troop of the municipal police. It starts at 22.00hrs on Thursdays between June and September.
Metro: Plaça d'Espanya.

♦♦♦
CASA AMATLLER
Passeig de Gràcia 41
The architect Puig i Cadafalch had Nordic Gothic inspiration when he began work on this apartment block in 1898. Note the finish, bold for its time, and the elegance of the ceramic tiling. With Gaudí's Casa Batlló and Domènech i Montaner's Casa Lleó-Morera, it makes up the so-called Manzana de Discordia, or Block of Discord, on which the different creations of the three famous Modernist architects can be studied.
Open: Tuesday to Saturday 10.00–14.00hrs; may be open some evenings.
Metro: Passeig de Gràcia.
Bus: 100 (stop 2).

♦♦♦
CASA BATLLÓ
Passeig de Gràcia 43
Both inside and outside, Gaudí showed his brilliance with natural forms when he remodelled this apartment block between 1904 and 1906. It has a wealth of undulating forms, different motifs, and bright and subtle colours in polychrome ceramics. The dominant decorative allusion is to Saint George and the Dragon. With a little imagination, the tile roof evokes the back of the dragon, and the bone-coloured parapets of the balconies suggest the skulls of its victims. Other interpretations are possible however.
Open: by arrangement, telephone 204 52 50. *Metro*: Passeig de Gràcia.
Bus: 100 (stop 2).

WHAT TO SEE

◆◆
CASA DE LA CIUTAT
Plaça de Sant Jaume
The City Hall, also known as the Ajuntament, has a neoclassical main façade. The original Flamboyant Gothic façade faces on to Carrer de la Ciutat. Inside there are a grand courtyard, a sweeping staircase, statues and richly decorated halls. The Saló de Cent (Hall of the Hundred) dates from the 14th century and was where Catalunya's leading notables met. The paintings by Josep M Sert in the Saló de Cróniques chronicle a Catalan expedition to the Far East in the 14th century.
Metro: Jaume I, Liceu, Plaça de Catalunya. *Bus*: 100 (stop 15).

◆◆◆
CASA LLEÓ-MORERA
Passeig de Gràcia 35
This apartment building was completed by Domènech i Montaner in 1905, with contributions from leading

Casa Mila, a wonderful carbuncle

sculptors, glaziers, joiners, painters and mosaic artists. They elaborately decorated the first floor apartment for the family which owned the building. This work has been carefully refurbished and the first floor is now the headquarters of the Patronat Municipal de Turisme.
Open: Monday to Saturday 09.00–14.30 and 15.30–17.30hrs.
Metro: Passeig de Gràcia.
Bus: 100 (stop 2).

◆◆
CASA MACAYA
Passeig de Sant Joan 108
A 1901 mansion by Puig i Cadalfach, the Casa Macaya has been converted to serve as a Centre Cultural de la Caixa de Pensions, and stages many good exhibitions and performances. The covered stairway is especially attractive, and the decorations include some notable sculpture.
Open: Tuesday to Saturday 11.00–14.00 and 16.00–20.00hrs; Sunday and holidays 10.00–15.00hrs. *Metro*: Verdaguer.

◆◆◆
CASA MILA
Passeig de Gràcia 92

Casa Mila is a big apartment building, which was Gaudí's last work of civil architecture. It was completed in 1910 and is also known as La Pedrera (the Stone Quarry) owing to the undulating mass of rough-chipped stone on its extensive façade. In 1984 UNESCO declared it to be a World Heritage Site. The Caixa de Catalunya, which now owns La Pedrera, has made it the headquarters of its cultural foundation. The building displays extraordinary innovation in its functional plan, the use of natural form and the combination of different materials. Gaudí made prolific use of wrought iron, and *trencadís* (broken marble) was ingeniously employed in the decoration of the four spiral columns which dominate the rooftop terrace. In order to have freedom in the layout of apartments on the five floors, Gaudí devised a method of minimising load-bearing walls and supporting the building on stone and brick columns combined with a web of steel. One of the interior patios is elliptical, the other circular. Spiral staircases lead from them to the floors and terrace. There are guided tours of the patios and terrace which last about 30 minutes.

Open: guided tours Monday to Friday 10.00, 11.00, 12.00, 13.00, 17.00, 18.00hrs; Saturday and Sunday 11.00, 12.00, 13.00hrs (except in August). *Metro*: Passeig de Gràcia, Diagonal. *Bus*: 100 (stop 2).

◆
CASA MUSEU GAUDÍ
Parc Güell

Gaudí did not design this house, but he lived in it from 1905 to 1926. It now exhibits mementos, furniture and drawings by the architect. See separate entry for Park Güell itself.

Open: March to November 10.00–14.00 and 16.00–19.00hrs. *Metro*: Lesseps. *Bus*: 100 (stop 4).

◆◆◆
CATEDRAL (LA SEU)
Plaça de la Seu

It was not until 1892 that the principal façade of La Seu, Barcelona's cathedral, was completed. The site first had an early Christian basilica, then a Romanesque church of which remains were incorporated into the present building. Although construction of the Gothic cathedral first started in 1298, most of the present building dates from the 14th century. The interior gives a great feeling of space with three high-vaulted naves, typical of the Catalan Gothic style. There are 29 side chapels, some of which are richly decorated. One has the Christ of Lepanto, used as the figurehead on the flagship of the fleet which defeated the Turks in the great sea battle of 1571. The choir shows fine medieval and Renaissance craftmanship in wood and marble.

In the crypt is the chapel of Santa Eulalia, one of the city's patron saints, to whom the cathedral is dedicated. Her sarcophagus is sculpted in alabaster, the work of an Italian artist in the 14th century. The cloister is a serene place where

WHAT TO SEE

La Seu's soaring Gothic nave

vaulted galleries enclose a garden with geese and a pond. *Ou com balla*, the dancing egg, bounces on the jet of a Gothic fountain in one of the chapels off the cloister; others have Gothic or Baroque decoration. Most notable of the exhibits in the Museu Capitular (cathedral museum) are a *Pietá* from the 15th century, a Gothic tabernacle and the throne of King Martin I, which is used during Corpus Christi processions.
Open: cathedral 07.00–13.30 and 16.00–19.30hrs; museum 11.00–13.00hrs. *Metro*: Jaume I, Liceu, Plaça de Catalunya. *Bus*: 100 (stops 1 and 15).

◆ CENTRE D'ART SANTA MÒNICA
La Rambla 7
Exhibitions of work in all sorts of art forms are presented in this modern exhibition centre of the Generalitat's department of culture. Its headquarters are in the 18th-century Palau March on the other side of La Rambla.
Open: Monday to Saturday 11.00–14.00 and 16.00–20.00hrs; Sunday and holidays 11.00–15.00hrs. *Metro*: Drassanes. *Bus*: 100 (stop 13).

◆◆ CENTRE PERMANENT D'ARTESANIA
Passeig de Gràcia 55
The Generalitat runs this centre to display the crafts, old and new, of Catalunya. It is the ideal place to get an idea of what is available and what to go looking for in the shops. Conveniently, the centre adjoins the prestigious shopping mall of Bulevar Rosa and the Centre d'Anticuaris, which offers a wide choice of shops selling antiques.
Open: shopping hours 09.00–1400 and 16.30–20.00hrs. *Metro*: Passeig de Gràcia, Diagonal. *Bus*: 100 (stop 2).

◆◆◆
CIUTAT VELLA DISTRICT (OLD TOWN)

The old town is the strongest magnet for first-time visitors to Barcelona, and it offers a rich mix of things to see and do. It is the area which once stood inside the city walls or just outside them, and from which the city grew in its 19th-century explosion of growth. Silent alleys in the Barri Gòtic contrast with the bustle of the broad La Rambla, where a multinational crowd constantly parades (a walk along La Rambla is an essential Barcelona experience). The parade goes on past the statue of Cristobal Colom and along the new Moll de la Fusta promenade beside the old harbour. Facing down La Rambla from Plaça de Catalunya, the barri of Casc Antic on the left (northeast) holds most interest. It includes the Barri Gòtic where an assembly of grand Gothic buildings, peaceful patios, narrow alleys and hidden squares created some 700 years ago remains a beguiling time warp. Some visitors like to read up on all the history linked with the old stones but others simply enjoy the resonant atmosphere. Restoration and maintenance has generally been thoughtful and the area has not been ruined by its popularity as a tourist attraction. Try to be around the Generalitat building at noon, when its bells play melodies, and if possible visit the Barri Gòtic again at night when it is floodlit.

Carrer Portaferrissa, leading left of La Rambla, is the principal shopping street in Ciutat Vella, with many good and varied stores. If shopping for food, do not miss the artistic display of foodstuffs in the Mercat de la Boqueria on La Rambla. There is no shortage of places in which to eat well in the Ciutat Vella, from basic budget to elegant and expensive. You can sip a drink and people-watch in the shadow of a church on Plaça Sant Josep Oriol, or enjoy rich chocolate from an old-time shop on nearby Carrer Petritxol. One of Barcelona's leading art galleries, Sala Parès, is also on this little street. Across the Via Laietana is the barri of Sant Pere-Ribera with more places of interest: Carrer Montcada is lined with handsome Gothic palaces which have been converted to museums (see Museu Picasso) or art galleries,

Barri Gòtic – a bridge to the past

like the Maeght. It leads to the 'cathedral of the sea', the big church of Santa Maria del Mar, which epitomises the grandeur of Catalan Gothic architecture. The surrounding area of El Born has good art galleries and interesting craft shops. Beyond the Passeig de Picasso lies the green Parc de la Ciutadella, a place for relaxing but also the site of the Museu d'Art Modern and the Zoo (Parc Zoològic). Fish restaurants are the main attraction of the harbourside area of Barceloneta. From here the cablecars of the Telefèric ride high across the harbour to the hill of Montjuïc.

◆◆◆
EIXAMPLE DISTRICT

'Eixample' means extension, and this district was laid out according to Ildefons Cerdà's

Passeig de Gràcia cuts a swathe

plan for the extension of the city in 1859. It was controversial at the time and it has not been universally liked since. His brief was to join the old city to the separate municipal areas of Gràcia, Sant Gervasi, Sarria and Sants. He planned a rigid grid of parallel streets 65 feet (20m) wide in which only two sides of each block would have buildings and the other two sides would be open to a central garden. The cut-off corners of intersections (*chaflanes*) were also to have been open spaces. The grid of his plan was retained but buildings were raised on all sides of the blocks, so that the Eixample is today very short of green spaces, although, happily, most of the streets are tree-lined. The monotony of the grid is broken by broader avenues like Gran Via de les Corts Catalanes and Avinguda

Diagonal. Passeig de Gràcia, three times the width of the Eixample's other streets, is the grandest of the city's boulevards. Parallel to Gràcia is the Rambla de Catalunya with its attractive central walkway and summertime open-air cafés. The part of the Eixample which holds most of interest for visitors lies between Gran Via de les Corts Catalanes, Diagonal and the parallels of Carrer Muntaner and Passeig de Sant Joan — that is, mostly the barri of Dreta de l'Eixample. Just beyond Passeig de Sant Joan to the north is the barri of Sagrada Família with Gaudí's unfinished cathedral as its centrepiece. At the end of the handsome Avinguda Gaudí is Domènech i Montaner's largest Modernist legacy, the Hospital de la Santa Creu i Sant Pau.

The Eixample's layout might seem boring but it is certainly not a boring part of Barcelona. It is studded with many jewels of Modernist architecture: brightest of them all is Gaudí's Casa Mila on Passeig de Gràcia; also on Passeig de Gràcia, the south block between Carrers Consell de Cent and d'Aragó, is the Manzana de Discordia (Block of Discord), with work by the three leading names among Modernist architects. On the next block, between Aragó and València, visit the Bulevar Rosa shopping mall, Centre Permanent d'Artesania and Centre d'Anticuaris, for a taste of the Eixample's many good shopping opportunities. The Vinçon store has modern design at fair prices; Carrer Consell de Cent, between Passeig de

Gràcia and Carrer Balmes, is lined with art galleries; and the Fundació Tàpies on Carrer d'Aragó is a new world class centre of contemporary culture. For eating and drinking, the Eixample offers every choice, including lots of *granjes* for sandwiches and salads, pizzerias and pastry shops along Rambla de Catalunya. At night, avant-garde Barcelona moves into the Eixample's designer music bars and discos.

◆◆◆
FONT DE CANALETES
Rambla de Canaletes
If you like Barcelona, make a point of taking a sip from this 19th-century cast-iron fountain which stands at the top of La Rambla near Plaça de Catalunya. Doing so is said to ensure that you will return to the city. Others say it makes you a true Barcelonan, but that is harder to achieve.
Metro: Plaça de Catalunya.
Bus: 100 (stop 1).

◆◆
FONTS LLUMINOSES DE MONTJUÏC
below the Palau Nacional, Montjuïc
The *fonts* are fountains, which are designed to make a spectacular show on certain days. Accompanied by music and changing colours, they appear to dance, in a routine which lasts for around an hour. The 'performances' take place on Thursday, Saturday, Sunday and holidays in summer, 22.00–23.00hrs; and on Saturday, Sunday and holidays in winter 21.00–22.00hrs.
Metro: Plaça d'Espanya.

WHAT TO SEE

◆◆◆
FUNDACIÓ MIRÓ

Plaça Neptú, Parc de Montjuïc
Joan Miró, Barcelonan born, died in 1983 at the age of 90, with a worldwide reputation as a painter, sculptor, ceramicist, engraver and designer. He also did significant works in textiles. Woman, the stars and birds are the most frequently repeated subjects. He received inspiration from diverse sources, such as the Surrealists of Paris and the artists of his much-loved Catalunya. In collaboration with his close friend, Joan Prats, Miró was in 1975 able to realise the plan of opening a centre dedicated to study and experimentation in contemporary art. Another friend, Josep Lluis Sert, designed the light and open building in which the Foundation is housed. Miró donated a substantial collection of his paintings, sculptures, textile creations, graphic works and drawings. Joan Prats also gave some of his Miró collection, and artists such as Tàpies and Calder contributed works of their own. Besides mounting exhibitions relating to Miró, the Foundation presents exhibitions of leading contemporary artists, lectures, film and video screenings, contemporary music performances and children's entertainments. Also here is the fascinating fountain of mercury, first created in 1937 by Alexander Calder for the Spanish Republic's stand at the Universal Exhibition in Paris. Adjoining the building is a recently established garden of sculptures. The library is well stocked with books and periodicals covering contemporary art, and there is a bookshop. This is a place where you could easily spend a good part of the day.

Open: Tuesday to Saturday 11.00–19.00hrs; Sunday and holidays 10.30–14.30hrs.
Funicular de Montjuïc. Bus: 61 from Plaça d'Espanya; 100 (stop 12).

Sculpture at the Fundació Miró

◆◆◆
FUNDACIÓ TÀPIES
Aragó 225

This is another contemporary art centre, named after the Catalan artist Antoni Tàpies. It opened in June 1990 in a converted Modernist building which was designed by Domènech i Montaner and previously owned by the publishing house of Montaner i Simon. Besides being known as an artist, Tàpies has been closely linked to civic causes of Barcelona and Catalunya, and been a vigorous supporter of democratic ideals and progressive ideas. His work shows his interest in different materials and symbolism, besides reflecting his preoccupation with the human condition. Some 325 of his paintings and sculptures and 3,000 graphic works, executed between 1948 and 1990, are on show. The artist's controversial sculpture, *Núvol i Cadira (Cloud and Chair)* sits atop the main façade. Temporary exhibitions of work by other contemporary artists are held in the additional exhibition space. Artistic and cultural events are presented in the auditorium and library. Antoni Tàpies and the Foundation's management have declared that this will be no mausoleum for works by Tàpies but a lively, questioning centre of contemporary culture.
Open: daily 11.00–20.00hrs.
Metro: Passeig de Gràcia.
Bus: 100 (stop 2).

◆◆
GENERALITAT
Plaça de Sant Jaume

The palace of the Generalitat, the regional government of Catalunya, is mostly a medieval Gothic building, despite its Greco-Roman style façade on the Plaça de Sant Jaume. The modern carving here represents Saint George slaying a dragon, and you can see another St George on the Gothic façade on Carrer del Bisbe Irurita. A passageway in Gothic style, but modern, runs across this street to connect the Generalitat palace with the 15th-century Casa dels Canonges. The palace's main courtyard, with its open stairway and double gallery, is a very beautiful example of civil architecture in the Catalan Gothic style, and the orangery is another attractive courtyard. Two other parts of the palace, the chapel and salon, are named after Sant Jordi (Saint George), the patron saint of Catalunya. The carillon in the palace's belltower plays at noon each day.

The Generalitat is open to visitors on 23 April, the feast day of Sant Jordi. Otherwise, you can visit on Saturdays and Sundays, but you must make a written request at least 15 days in advance. Enquire at a tourist office for more information on visits.
Metro: Jaume I. *Bus*: 100 (stop 15).

◆◆
GRÀCIA DISTRICT

The atmosphere of a village lingers in the warren of streets within the barri of Gràcia, which has been known for its independent, sometimes revolutionary, spirit. There are cheaper eating places and

WHAT TO SEE

shops and some night-time venues which are an alternative to the modishness elsewhere. Its neighbouring barri, Vallcarca, has two of Barcelona's most delightful and interesting parks: Modernist Park Güell and modern Parc de la Creueta del Coll, created out of a former quarry.

◆

GRAN TEATRE DEL LICEU
Sant Pau 1 (La Rambla)
First opened in 1847, this sumptuous opera house is one of the world's biggest, and has long been the premier venue for opera in Spain. It also presents an annual season of ballet. Guided tours with commentaries in Catalan, Castilian, English and French last around 30 minutes.
Open: guided tours Monday to Friday 11.30 and 12.15hrs for groups of up to five. For larger groups contact the Public Relations Department (tel: 318 9122).
Metro: Liceu. *Bus:* 100 (stops 1 and 13).

◆

HOMENAJE A PICASSO
Passeig de Picasso
This tribute of one artist to a greater, Antoni Tàpies to Pablo Picasso, was executed in 1983 as a feature of the remodelled Passeig de Picasso, which borders the Parc de la Ciutadella. It is a curious, provocative creation composed of everyday objects in a glass case, with water streaming down the sides.
Metro: Arc del Triomf. *Bus:* 100 (stop 14).

◆◆◆

HOSPITAL DE LA SANTA CREU I SANT PAU
north end of Avinguda Gaudí
Many visitors to Barcelona never see the city's largest complex of Modernist buildings, some 20 in all, designed by Lluís Domènech i Montaner and completed by his son Pere in 1930. Domènech did not favour Cerdà's rigid plan for the Eixample district, and within the spacious gardens of the hospital he arranged his buildings at an angle to the blocks of the Eixample. Tunnels connect the buildings, many of which, especially the entrance building, have Mudéjar style design and decoration. This interesting hospital complex can be viewed from the public areas.
Metro: Sagrada Família, Guinardo. *Bus:* 100 (stop 3).

◆

INSTITUT I JARDÍ BOTANIC
Parc de Montjuïc
A new botanic garden, developed in phases on a site between the Olympic Stadium and the Castell de Montjuïc (the castle). Plants are grouped according to geographical origin and ecology. The scheme includes aquatic plants, in ponds on three levels. Visitors can find out about the garden in the reception centre at the entrance near the Olympic Stadium.
Open: Monday to Saturday, summer 15.00–19.00hrs; winter 15.00–17.00hrs; Sunday and holidays all year 09.00–14.00hrs.
Bus: 61 from Plaça d'Espanya; 100 (stop 12).

♦♦♦
LA RAMBLA (LAS RAMBLAS)

If you could only visit one of Barcelona's sights, you could do far worse than La Rambla, the long street running from Plaça de Catalunya to Plaça Portal de la Pau, by the sea. La Rambla is also known as Las Ramblas, because it is formed by five linked streets, all called Rambla-something. The individual names are Canaletes, Estudis, Sant Josep, Caputxins and Santa Monica. Rambla means torrent in Arabic and that is what flowed here until it was paved over. A central walkway with plane trees was first made in the 1770s, and by the late 1850s La Rambla had become the city's most fashionable boulevard. It is no longer the most prestigious place to live, but it is the most cosmopolitan and most animated street in the city, with cafés, news kiosks and strolling people providing an endlessly interesting free show. See also **Walks**.

Metro: Plaça de Catalunya, Liceu, Drassanes. *Bus*: 100 (stops 1 and 13).

♦
MERCAT CONCEPCIÓ

on the block between Aragó, València, Bruc and Girona
Mercat Concepció is a city market, similar to La Boqueria but smaller. The setting is handy for residents of the Eixample.
Metro: Girona, Passeig de Gràcia. *Bus*: 100 (stop 2).

♦♦♦
MERCAT DE SANT JOSEP (LA BOQUERIA)

La Rambla
Barcelona has a number of good food markets spread through its city districts. This one has been operating since 1836 and is the

A torrent of flowers in La Rambla

overall favourite — a huge, generally spotless expanse of foodstuffs of every imaginable sort, arranged in elaborate and colourful displays. Fish, exotic fruit and homely vegetables become art here. From early in the morning to the evening, the place bustles with housewives and restaurateurs searching for their needs among the many stalls. There are also bars and eating places for a drink, snack or meal while you watch the scene. El Pinocho, just right of the entrance, has become *the* place for fashionable revellers to greet the day with breakfast after an all-night stint at bars and discos.

Metro: Liceu. *Bus*: 100 (stops 1 and 13).

♦♦
MOLL DE LA FUSTA

This new seafront promenade has been developed as part of the city's *nou urbanisme* programme. It used to be a timber wharf, but now helps to open up the city to the sea. The design incorporates an underpass for the coastal ring road (Cinturó del Litoral), an underground carpark and a raised pedestrian terrace with bars, restaurants and views of the harbour and sea. Stairs lead down to the cobbled wharf which is graced by palm trees. It makes a pleasant place to take a stroll or sit on a bench and watch the world go by. On warm evenings it gets thronged with Barcelonans taking the air and displaying their style.

Metro: Drassanes. *Bus*: 100 (stops 13 and 14).

♦♦♦
MONTJUÏC DISTRICT

Montjuïc is the hill above the harbour on the west side of the city. There was already a settlement here when the Romans arrived, and it became a ceremonial site which they named Mons Jovis, the Hill of Jupiter. The northern side of the hill has been progressively landscaped since the late 19th century, to become an extensive park area of more than 500 acres (202 hectares). It was for the 1929 Universal Exhibition that the park acquired its gardens, palaces, pavilions, sports facilities, exhibition halls, fountains and the Poble Espanyol — all of which help to make Montjuïc an out-of-the-ordinary urban green space. It can be reached by cablecar from Barceloneta, or from Moll Barcelona in the harbour. Other public transport approaches to Montjuïc are by funicular from Avinguda de Paral-lel and by bus from Plaça d'Espanya. From the funicular station another cablecar rides over the beautiful Jardins de Mossèn Jacint Verdaguer and Parc d'Atraccions de Montjuïc (amusement park) to the Castell de Montjuïc. Now dominating the hill more than the castle is the Anella Olímpica (Olympic Ring), the principal site of the 1992 Olympic Games, with the Estadi Olímpic, Palau d'Esports Sant Jordi and Complex Esportiu Bernat Picornell. These and other sports venues, and the new INEF sports university, make Montjuïc a paradise for the sports enthusiast. It has its cultural side too however: see separate entries for the superb collection of Romanesque art in the Museu d'Art de Catalunya and the contemporary arts centre of the Fundació Miró. The Mercat de les Flors theatre, a converted flower market, and, in summer, the Teatre Grec offer a variety of good productions. In the Poble Espanyol, anyone with an interest in the architecture of Spain can quickly get an idea of regional and period variations from the reproduction façades of many of the country's most famous buildings. There are also craftshops, bars, eating places and late-night haunts to enjoy. Near by is the Pavelló Barcelona, a reconstruction of the architectural gem first designed by Mies van der Rohe. On Saturday and Sunday nights there is a magical display of the fountains below the Palau Nacional; on Thursday nights in summer, horsemen of the municipal police present their Carousel. At any time there are green spaces for lazing or exercising, with broad vistas across the city.

Standing proud: Monument a Colom

◆◆
MONUMENT A COLOM
Plaça Portal de la Pau
An iron column of some 165 feet (50m) supports the statue of Cristobal Colom (Christopher Columbus) which was raised for the Universal Exhibition of 1888. A lift takes you to the viewing platform for panoramic views across the city and harbour. *Open*: Summer (around 20 June to 20 September), daily 09.00–21.00hrs; rest of the year, Tuesday to Saturday 10.00–14.00

and 15.30–18.30hrs, Sunday and holidays 10.00–19.00hrs. *Metro*: Drassanes. *Bus*: 100 (stop 13).

◆
MUSEU ARQUEOLÒGIC
Passeig Santa Madrona, Parc de Montjuïc
The exhibits date from the early colonising of Catalunya and the rest of Iberia, including lots of Roman pieces from Empúries on the Costa Brava. Also here are items of the Talayot culture from Mallorca, and a collection of Punic (Carthaginian) finds from Ibiza. *Open*: Tuesday to Saturday 09.30–13.00 and 16.00–19.00hrs; Sunday and holidays 09.30–14.00hrs. *Bus*: 61 from Plaça d'Espanya; 100 (stop 12).

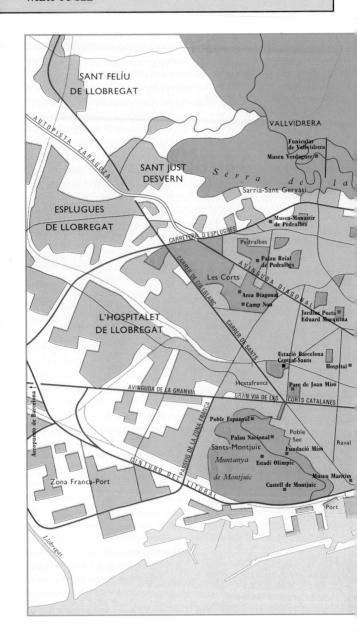

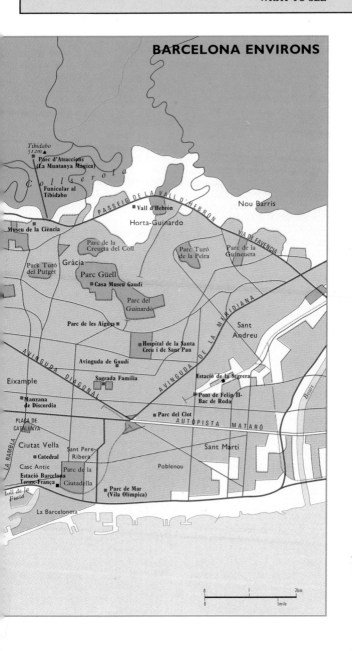

BARCELONA ENVIRONS

Tibidabo
512m ▲
Parc d'Atraccions
(La Muntanya Màgica)

C o l l s e r o l a

Funicular al
Tibidabo

PASSEIG DE LA VALL D'HEBRON

Vall d'Hebrón

Nou Barris

Museu de la Ciència

Horta-Guinardó

VIA DE FAVENCIA

Parc de la
Creueta del Coll

Parc Turó
de la Peira

Parc de la
Guineueta

Park Turó
del Putget

Gràcia

Parc Güell

Casa Museu Gaudí

Parc del
Guinardó

Sant
Andreu

Parc de les Aigües

AVINGUDA DE LA MERIDIANA

Hospital de la Santa
Creu i de Sant Pau

AVINGUDA DIAGONAL

Avinguda de Gaudí

Eixample

Sagrada Família

AVINGUDA DE LA MERIDIANA

Estació de la Sagrera

Manzana
de Discòrdia

Pont de Felip II-
Bac de Roda

Besòs

PLAÇA DE
CATALUNYA

Parc del Clot

AUTOPISTA MATARÓ

LA RAMBLA

Ciutat Vella

Catedral

Sant Pere-
Ribera

Sant Martí

Casc Antic

Parc de la
Ciutadella

Poblenou

Estació Barcelona
Terme-França

Moll de la
Fusta

Parc de Mar
(Vila Olímpica)

La Barceloneta

0   1   2km
0   1mile

WHAT TO SEE

♦♦♦

MUSEU D'ART DE CATALUNYA

Palau Nacional, Parc de Montjuïc

The Palau Nacional was the principal construction for the 1929 Universal Exhibition, before becoming the home of the city's most impressive museum. Great works of Catalan art are kept here, and there has been much controversy about the building's renovation and better adaptation as the showpiece of Catalunya. An agreement was reached in January 1990 between Barcelona's municipal authority and the Catalan government to go ahead with the first phase of renovation and remodelling at an estimated cost of 4,000 million pesetas. The architect appointed was the Italian Gae Aulenti. The museum's greatest treasure is its outstanding collection of Catalan Romanesque art, made up of frescoes, painted wood panels and sculptures, some of which date from the 10th century. Most of the works were saved from abandoned religious buildings in the early part of this century by concerned Catalans, such as the architect and politician Puig i Cadalfach. Bright colours were used in the murals and panels, and both painting and sculpture show Byzantine influence in their stiffly poised, neatly arranged representations of people. Apart from giving colour and decoration to severe interiors, the purpose of this art was partly to teach, and it still makes a vivid impression today. The collection of Catalan Gothic art is also strong and is supplemented by Gothic works from other parts of Spain. In painting this period is distinguished by the use of gold for embossing backgrounds (*esgrafiado*) and for raised clothing and haloes (*estofado*). The rest of the museum's collection consists of baroque and Renaissance works, less extensive and remarkable than the Romanesque and Gothic sections, but including work by El Greco and Zurbarán. *Open*: Tuesday to Sunday 09.00–14.00hrs. *Metro*: Plaça d'Espanya. *Bus*: 100 (stop 10).

♦♦

MUSEU D'ART MODERN

Plaça d'Armes, Parc de la Ciutadella

Catalan artists such as Fortuny, Nonell, Casals, Rusinyol and Gargallo dominate this collection of 19th- and 20th-century art. It includes paintings, sculptures, drawings, engravings and decorative art. *Open*: Tuesday to Saturday 09.00–19.30hrs; Sunday and holidays 09.00–14.00hrs. *Metro*: Arc del Triomf. *Bus*: 100 (stop 14).

♦

MUSEU ETNOLÒGIC

Passeig de Santa Madrona, Parc de Montjuïc

Artefacts from many of the world's cultures can be seen here, and the collection is especially strong on those from the Philippines and New Guinea. The museum also presents temporary exhibitions. *Open*: Tuesday to Saturday 09.00–20.30hrs; Monday 15.00–20.30hrs; Sunday and holidays 09.00–14.00hrs. *Bus*: 61 from Plaça d'Espanya; 100 (stop 12).

◆◆◆
MUSEU FREDERIC MARÉS
Plaça de Sant Iu
Frederic Marés was a sculptor, traveller and collector extraordinary. The museum was started in 1946 and has two totally different sections. One part shows sculptures from pre-Roman times to the present century; the other section, the 'sentimental museum', has a fascinating magpie collection from daily life, spanning the period from the 15th to the early 20th century.
Open: Tuesday to Saturday 09.00–14.00 and 16.00–19.00hrs; Sunday and holidays 09.00–14.00hrs. *Metro:* Jaume I. *Bus:* 100 (stop 15).

◆◆◆
MUSEU D'HISTÒRIA DE LA CIUTAT
Plaça del Rei
The museum of the history of the city is a good place to start your discovery of Barcelona. It is housed in the Casa Clariana-Padellás, a Gothic building which was moved stone by stone from another site to complete the Plaça del Rei. In its cellars are the excavated remains of buildings from Roman Barcelona, and the exhibits in the museum itself include plans by Cerdà for the city's mid-19th-century extension, the Eixample. There are also views of the city as it was in former times, among other items illustrating Barcelona's past.
Open: Tuesday to Saturday 09.00–20.30hrs; Sunday and holidays 09.00–13.30hrs. *Metro:* Jaume I. *Bus:* 100 (stop 15).

◆◆◆
MUSEU MARÍTIM
Plaça Portal de la Pau
Medieval shipyards called the Drassanes, dating from the 13th century, have been well restored to create this museum chronicling maritime history. Pride of place is held by a replica of *La Real*, the flagship of Don Juan of Austria, brother of Philip II, who destroyed the Turkish fleet in the battle of Lepanto in 1571. Many Catalans served in Don Juan's fleet.
Open: Tuesday to Saturday 10.00–14.00 and 16.00–19.00hrs; Sunday and holidays 10.00–14.00hrs. *Metro:* Drassanes. *Bus:* 100 (stop 13).

Frederic Marés' collection

WHAT TO SEE

◆◆◆
MUSEU MONESTIR DE PEDRALBÉS
Baixada Monestir 9

Queen Elisenda, wife of Jaume II who ordered the building of Barcelona's cathedral, founded the monastery in the 14th century and is buried here. This is one of the gems of Catalan Gothic architecture — many people prefer it to the more intimidating cathedral. The multi-level cloister is the best in Barcelona, with the slender columns and delicate arches typical of the period; and murals by a leading artist of the time, Ferrer Bassa, decorate Sant Miquel chapel. There are echoes of past monastic life in the kitchen, refectory and chapter house, and the nun's church can also be visited. A display in one room gives an account of the Catalan royal line. If the bustle of downtown Barcelona is becoming wearing, a journey to this monastery for peace and reflection is an ideal

Arcaded terrace, Museu Picasso

antidote. It lies outside the city centre, but is worth the journey. *Open:* Tuesday to Sunday 09.30–14.00hrs. *Metro:* Reina Elisenda. *Bus:* 22, 64, 75, 100 (stop 7).

◆
MUSEU DE LA MÚSICA
Diagonal 373

The collection of musical instruments is only part of the attraction — the museum building itself is also full of interest. Puig i Cadalfach completed the Modernist renovation of this mansion in 1904. Instruments from the 16th century onwards are grouped by type, and there is biographical documentation on Catalan composers.
Open: Tuesday to Sunday 09.00–14.00hrs. *Metro:* Diagonal. *Bus:* 100 (stop 2).

◆◆◆
MUSEU PICASSO
Carrer Montcada 15–19

People may consider you a philistine if you have been to Barcelona and not visited this museum; another reason for

visiting is to see the beautiful 15th-century Palau Berenguer d'Aguilar and adjoining Palau Castellet which constitute the museum. But it is Picasso's work that draws the crowds, who often have to form long lines. This is one of the world's two museums devoted solely to Picasso − the other is in Paris − and is one of Barcelona's top attractions. Jaume Sabartes, Picasso's long-time secretary and friend, donated the bulk of the collection in 1960 so that the Barcelona municipality could start the museum. It includes paintings, drawings, ceramics, and graphics, and is strongest on the artist's early years. There are drawings and paintings from his Andalucian childhood and from his teenage years in Barcelona, as well as portraits of his parents and work he did at the Llotja school of art. The most popular and familiar picture here is probably his *Harlequin*. In 1968 Picasso donated a series of 58 canvases based on Velázquez's *Las Meninas*. Pablo Ruíz Picasso was born in Málaga in 1881 and moved to Barcelona in 1895 when his father took up a teaching position at the Llotja. From 1899 until he permanently left Barcelona for Paris in 1904 he was a member of the artistic group which gathered at Els Quatre Gats café in Carrer Montsió. Santiago Rusinyol, Ramon Casals and Isidre Nonell whose works are seen in the Museu d'Art Modern were leading lights of the group. Picasso's first exhibition, based on themes of Barcelonan life, was held at Els Quatre Gats.

The museum also hosts good temporary exhibitions.
Open: Tuesday to Sunday and holidays 10.00–20.00hrs.
Metro: Jaume I. *Bus*: 100 (stops 14 and 15).

◆
MUSEU TÈXTIL I DE LA INDUMENTÀRIA
Carrer Montcada 12–14
The museum of textiles and costume is more interesting than you might expect, with tapestries and clothing from medieval to modern times, and some much earlier pieces too. The exhibits are in chronological order in three main sections − textiles, lace and garments. There is also an interesting collection of dolls and machinery. As so often, the building alone is worth a visit.
Open: Tuesday to Saturday 09.00–14.00 and 16.30–19.00hrs; Sunday and holidays 09.00–14.00hrs. *Metro*: Jaume I. *Bus*: 100 (stops 14 and 15).

◆
MUSEU DE ZOOLOGIA
Parc de la Ciutadella, Passeig Picasso
Lluís Domènech i Montaner designed the building − the Castell dels Tres Dragons − to be a café-restaurant for the 1888 Universal Exhibition. On the upper floor there is a permanent display of stuffed animals, reptiles and birds. Temporary exhibitions on zoological, biological and environmental themes are held in the lower hall, and are worth investigating.
Open: Tuesday to Sunday 09.00–14.00hrs. *Metro*: Arc del Triomf. *Bus*: 100 (stop 14).

◆◆◆
PALAU GÜELL

Carrer Nou de la Rambla 3–5
The large mansion was built between 1886 and 1888 for the Güell family and was the first big architectural project in which Antoni Gaudí expressed his individuality. The building is an interpretation of the Gothic style, with Moorish elements. In the narrow street it is difficult to get a good view of it and appreciate its scale. You can however see the severe façade, relieved somewhat by the first-floor balcony, the arches of the two doors, sinuous door grilles and the Catalan coats of arms in wrought iron. Inside, the principal rooms are arranged around a central well which holds the main salon. This has both an organ and a closet altar, and doubles as a concert room

and chapel. The decoration is rich and varied – marble columns, parabolic arches, precious woods, appliqués of ivory and mother of pearl, fascinating iron work, paintings by Aleix Clapès and fine pieces of furniture are all used here. In 1984 Unesco classified the Palau Güell as a World Heritage Site. It houses the small collection of the Museu de les Arts de l'Espectacle (theatre museum), which also stages temporary exhibitions related to the theatre.

Open: Tuesday to Saturday 10.00–13.00 and 17.00–19.00hrs.
Metro: Liceu. *Bus*: 100 (stop 13).

◆◆◆
PALAU DE LA MÚSICA CATALANA

Sant Pere Més Alt
The most glorious confection of Catalan Modernism was completed in 1908. Domènech i

Green peace in Parc de la Ciutadella

Montaner worked with sculptors Arnau and Gargallo and other master craftsmen in ceramics, glass and wood to create what must be the world's most fanciful, and diverting, concert hall. Few surfaces are left untouched – the elaborate decoration drips off the ceilings as well as the walls. Domènech set out to achieve an integration of art forms in his celebration of music, and he achieved it in a densely ornate but harmonious whole. Almost everybody seeing the interior for the first time is awestruck: some find it horribly excessive and tasteless, more fall instantly in love with the place, but few remain indifferent. The narrowness of the street makes it difficult to appreciate the elaborate façade, but it is really the interior which must be seen. Just looking through the glass doors into the foyer will provide some idea of the rest, but undoubtedly the best time to experience it is during a concert, when the whole place takes on a vibrant atmosphere. The Palau opened with performances by the Berlin Philharmonic, and has been graced by the world's leading orchestras, choirs and soloists ever since.
Metro: Urquinaona.

◆
PALAU REIAL DE PEDRALBÉS
Avinguda Diagonal 686
The city commissioned the Italian Renaissance style palace and gave it with the extensive park to King Alfonso XIII in the 1920s. It is packed with fine furniture, paintings, sculptures

and royal memorabilia, and also houses the Museu Ceramica and Museu d'Arts Decoratives. The park includes a formal garden.
Open: Tuesday to Friday 10.00–13.00 and 16.00–18.00hrs; Saturday, Sunday and holidays 10.00–13.00hrs (check at a tourist office). *Metro*: Palau Reial. *Bus*: 7, 75, 100 (stop 7).

◆
PALAU DE LA VIRREINA
La Rambla 99
'La Virreina' refers to the wife of the Viceroy of Peru. She had the good fortune to enjoy the rococo palace which her husband had commissioned, but he died soon after its completion in 1778. It is the headquarters of the Ajuntament's department of culture. The exhibition rooms have changing shows, and there is a shop selling books, posters, cards and the like. Tickets for municipally sponsored shows and events can usually be bought here.
Metro: Liceu. *Bus*: 100 (stop 1).

◆◆
PARC DE LA CIUTADELLA
Passeig de Picasso, Passeig de Pujades
The name of the park is derived from the huge fort built by Felipe V, which Barcelonans happily demolished and replaced with gardens designed by Josep Fonseré in 1873. The Catalan Parliament and the Museu d'Art Modern now occupy the fort's arsenal building. As principal site for the Universal Exhibition of 1888 the park received additional buildings, such as Domènech i Montaner's Castell dels Tres

WHAT TO SEE

Dragons. The French landscape designer Forestier laid out the Plaça d'Armes, where you can see the beautiful *El Desconsol* sculpture by the Modernist Josep Llimona. Other things to look out for are the Umbracle, a structure of wood and iron now filled with tropical plants, and the steel and glass Hivernacle, which is used for exhibitions. The over-wrought design of the park's monumental fountain was by Fonséré, but it is more famous today because the young Gaudí worked on its construction. The northeast corner of the park is occupied by the zoo (see separate entry). *Metro*: Arc del Triomf, Barceloneta. *Bus*: 100 (stop 14).

♦♦
PARC DEL CLOT

An old railway site has been imaginatively converted here by the architects Dani Freixes and Vicenç Miranda. Instead of completely demolishing the railway roundhouse which occupied most of the site, they have incorporated remains of its walls and arches, and its tall chimney, into the park's design. The *clot* (hole) has become a playing field, and there are various other pleasing features, such as a bridge walkway, a pergola, trellises and sculpture by Bryan Hunt.
Metro: Clot.

♦♦♦
PARC DE LA CREUETA DEL COLL

La Creueta was a quarry in the lower folds of the Collserola hills, and has been converted into a leisure park by architects

David Mackay and Josep Martorell. It has a lake with an artificial beach which is used for swimming in the summer, and in winter there are boats for hire. Paths run through woods with viewing points across the city, and inevitably sculpture is an important feature. The large piazza has a suspended sculpture by the Basque Eduardo Chillida, *Elogi de l'aigua* (*In Praise of Water*), and there are others by Ellsworth Kelly and Roy Lichtenstein. *Metro*: Penitents. *Bus*: 100 (stop 5).

♦♦♦
PARC DE L'ESPANYA INDUSTRIAL

adjoining Estació Sants
This is a concrete park, created on the site of an old textile factory. The design by architects Luis Peña Ganchegui and Francesc Rius i Camps was controversial when unveiled in 1982, and became even more so when the public were admitted three years later. At first sight the upper level of the park is intimidating and reminiscent of a prison: there are 10 tall towers with spotlights and viewing platforms which look like sentry posts. A softer image takes over on the lower level, which has a lake, lawns, paths, trees and a variety of sculptures (from classical to avant-garde) by leading Catalan artists. Andrés Nagel created the fun sculpture of *Drac de Sant Jordi* (*St George's Dragon*), much appreciated by children. This is a park which will either impress or depress.
Metro: Sants. *Bus*: 100 (stop 9).

♦♦♦
PARC GÜELL
d'Olot

Gaudí's patron Eusebi Güell had
the original idea for the park: it
was to be an English-style
garden suburb, which would
have had 60 residences. Only
two houses were built, however,
as the project failed, and the
property was taken over by the
municipality in 1923. Gaudí's
contribution between 1900 and
1914 was to design and direct
the construction of the
infrastructure, and he did so in
his unmistakable style. Sinuous
lines and natural forms,
mythological allusions, broken
marble, spiral-shaped towers
and giant lizards are all used
here. It was clearly his intention
that the constructions —
stairways, viaducts, ramps and
buildings — should have an
organic look. The best bit is the
three-tiered construction which
he created for quite mundane
purposes: a water cistern with
what was to have been the
market place above it, and a
large plaça above that. The hall
for the market place has 84
columns, based on a Classical
style but eccentric, supporting
decorative domes. Gaudí's plan
was that water would drain from
the plaça down the interior of
the columns to the cistern — an
example of his innovative
technical solutions. A serpentine
balustrade and bench defines
the limits of the plaça, from
which there are wide views
across the city. Gaudí's
collaborator, Josep Jujol, was
largely responsible for this
bench, which is one of the city's
most photographed images. The

Parc Güell, Gaudí's suburban dream

park was declared a World
Heritage Site by Unesco in 1984.
See also Casa Museu Gaudí.
Metro: Vallcarca. *Bus*: 24, 25, 100
(stop 4).

♦
PARC DE JOAN MIRÓ
Tarragona, Aragó

There used to be an abbattoir
on this site, but despite such
unpromising beginnings, the
park is popular with local
people. Visitors come to see the
elevated concrete area with its
bright and suggestive sculpture
by Joan Miró, *Dona i Ocell*
(*Woman and Bird*), which rises
to 70 feet (22m).
Metro: Sants, Tarragona or Plaça
d'Espanya. *Bus*: 100 (stop 9).

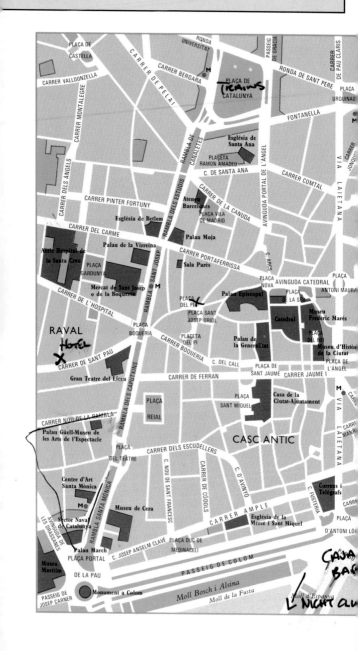

CENTRAL BARCELONA

CARRER DE ROGER DE LLURIA
Casa Calvet
CARRER DEL BRUC
CARRER DE GIRONA
CARRER DE BAILEN
PASSEIG DE SANT JOAN
CARRER DE NAPOLS

CARRER D'AUSIÀS MARC
CARRER D'AUSIÀS MARC
CARRER DE

RONDA DE SANT PERE
CARRER D'ALÍBEI
ROGER DE FLOR
CARRER DE

CARRER DE TRAFALGAR
CARRER D'ALÍBEI
CARRER DE RIBES

D'ORTIGOSA
CARRER DE TRAFALGAR
AVINGUDA VILANOVA

Palau de la Música
C. MENDEZ NÚÑEZ
Sant Pere

CARRER SANT PERE MÉS ALT
Arc del Triomf
M

PLAÇA SANT PERE
CARRER REC COMTAL
CARRER DELS ALMOGÀVERS

CARRER SANT PERE MÉS BAIX
Palau Justicia

PLAÇETA COMERÇ
CARRER PORTAL NOU

AVINGUDA ANCESC CAMBÓ
CARRER FONOLLAR
CARRER BUENAVENTURA MUÑOZ

Mercat Santa Caterina
PLAÇA SANT AGUSTÍ VELL
PASSEIG DE LLUIS COMPANYS

CARRER CARDERS
CARRER DEL COMERÇ

C. CORDERS
C. TANTARANTANA
PASSEIG DE PUJADES

PLAÇA PONS I CLERCH
Museu de Zoologia

CARRER DE LA PRINCESA
SANT PERE-
Parc de la Ciutadella

PASSEIG DE PICASSO

Museu Picasso
CARRER DEL REC
CARRER FUSINA
Museu de Geologia

Museu Tèxtil i de la Indumentària
CARRER MONTCADA
RIBERA

Església de Santa Maria del Mar
PLAÇA COMERCIAL
Mercat del Born

PLAÇA SANTA MARIA
PASSEIG DEL BORN
CARRER DE LA RIBERA
Museu d'Art Modern

C. BONAIRE
PLAÇA D'ARMES

CONSOLAT DE MAR
Parlament de Catalunya

Llotja
PLAÇA
AVINGUDA MARQUÉS DE L'ARGENTERA

PASSEIG ISABEL II
DE PALAU
PASSEIG CIRCUNVAL·LACIÓ

URALLA
Estació Barcelona Terme-França
Parc Zoològic

M

Dipòsit
PLAÇA DE PAU VILA
AVINGUDA D' ICÀRIA

0   100   200   300 metres

WHAT TO SEE

◆
PARC DEL POETA EDUARD MARQUINA

Avinguda Pau Casals
Also known as Turó Parc, it makes a good place to relax awhile in this uptown district. There are formal gardens, children's playgrounds and an open-air theatre, plus sculptures by Catalans, including a monument at the entrance in memory of Pau Casals.
Bus: 7, 66.

◆◆◆
PAVELLÓ BARCELONA

Avinguda del Marqués de Comillas, Montjuïc
The Bauhaus architect Mies van der Rohe designed this plain and simple building as the German pavilion for the Universal Exhibition of 1929. Although it is widely regarded as one of the classic buildings of this century it was taken down and had to be reconstructed in the mid-1980s. Marble, onyx, chrome plate and glass were the materials used, and there is a copy of a bronze by Georg Kolbe.
Metro: Plaça d'Espanya. *Bus*: 100 (stop 10).

◆
PEDRALBÉS DISTRICT

This barri of luxury housing has one of Barcelona's unsung glories: the 14th-century (Museu) Monestir de Pedralbés, which strongly evokes the glory of medieval Barcelona. Pedralbés also has the Palau Reial and, with the barri of Les Corts across Avinguda Diagonal, the campus of Barcelona's university.

◆◆
PLAÇA DE CATALUNYA

Everyone arrives at this square sooner or later in their time in Barcelona. It is the connecting hub between the Ciutat Vella and the Eixample, and is also the centre of the city's transport network – for example, this is the starting point (stop 1) for the Bus Turístic, Number 100. It is also a venue for public entertainments, meetings and rallies. The plaça as you see it today was completed in 1927. Notable among its statues are two on the western side, by Clará and Gargallo, *La Diosa* and *El Pastor Tocando el Caramillo* respectively. Ornate lampstands are another feature, and some people consider the star in the central pavement to represent the centre of Catalunya. If you want to rest and reflect, rent a *cadira de lloquer* (chair) and watch the world go by.
Metro: Plaça de Catalunya. *Bus*: 100 (stop 1).

◆
PLAÇA PAISOS CATALANS

in front of Estació Sants
This is one of the *espais urbans* (urban spaces) which leave many people bemused. Architects Piñon, Viaplana and Miralles came up with a bold plan to deal with a difficult space – they unexpectedly filled it with unusual structures. A serpentine pagoda, a broad, tall canopy, podiums without statues, a series of fountains, a play area for children, and more.
Metro: Sants. *Bus*: 100 (stop 9).

◆◆◆
PLAÇA DEL REI
Barri Gòtic

The first sight of this noble square is unforgettable — it can hardly have changed since medieval times, when the city was at the height of its power. In fact, the 17th-century Casa Clariana Padellás, on the right as you enter the plaça is a newcomer moved stone by stone from elsewhere and rebuilt to complete the scene. It houses the Museu d'Història de la Ciutat (see separate entry) and its terrace gives a good view of the old buildings (*open*: Tuesday to Saturday 09.00-20.30hrs, Sunday 09.00-13.30hrs). A wide semicircle of steps leads to the 14th-century Capel de Santa Agueda which forms the right side of the plaça. The chapel's interior has recently been restored and its prize possession is an altarpiece, the *Condestable*, by Jaume Huguet. The same steps give access to the Palau Real Mayor, an enlargement of what used to be the residence of the Counts of Barcelona, which forms the top of the plaça. The exterior has tall double arches and recessed windows and you can see Rei Martí, a 16th-century skyscraper, rising behind. Inside is the lofty, handsome Saló del Tinell, where once the Spanish Inquisition sat and where today a variety of exhibitions and other events is held. The fourth side of the plaça is formed by the Catalan Gothic façade of the Palau del Lloctinent, built in 1549 for the representative in Catalunya of the king in Madrid. During warmer months, the Plaça del Rei is a venue for musical and theatrical events.
Metro: Jaume I. *Bus*: 100 (stop 15).

◆
PLAÇA REIAL
off La Rambla

The rectangle of neoclassical arcaded buildings was built in the last century, on the site of Barcelona's Capuchin convent. Having acquired a very sleazy reputation, it has now been restored to its former elegance, but the police are permanently on patrol to ensure that it does not become its old, intimidating self. It retains a certain seediness however. The Plaça Reial is graced by tall palm trees, two street lamps by Gaudí and a fountain showing the Three Graces. Numerous bars line the arcades and their tables and chairs spill out into the open air in summer. On Sundays this is the busy scene of a stamp and coin market.
Metro: Liceu. *Bus*: 100 (stop 13).

Rei Marti over Plaça del Rei

WHAT TO SEE

◆◆◆
POBLE ESPANYOL
Avinguda del Marqués de Comillas, Montjuïc
The *poble* (village) was built for the Universal Exhibition of 1929, and portrays the architecture of Spain's regions by reproducing the façades of notable buildings. The village has been extensively renovated and refurbished and is now managed by a private company with an eye to Catalunya's tourist industry. It is an undeniably touristy place but even the most hardened travel snob could warm to it. Besides seeing the various architectural styles and being temporarily transported to other parts of Spain, you can visit artisan workshops and artists' studios, handicraft and souvenir shops, restaurants specialising in regional food and drink, bars, music bars, nightclubs and a disco. There is also an audio-visual on Barcelona, and some kind of show is usually being presented in the main square. *Open*: 09.00-02.00hrs and later at weekends. *Metro*: Plaça d'Espanya. *Bus*: 100 (stop 10).

◆
PONT DE FELIP II – BAC DE RODA
connecting Felip II and Bac de Roda
This 420-foot (128m) bridge-sculpture by engineer and architect Santiago Calatrava should be seen by anybody with an interest in architecture and urban planning. It is one of the most outstanding examples of Barcelona's *nou urbanisme* programme.
Metro: Clot.

◆
RECINTE FIRAL
Plaça d'Espanya, Montjuïc
Barcelona has a full annual agenda of trade and consumer affairs, which are held in this extensive fair complex. Most of it was constructed for the Universal Exhibition of 1929. Some events are open to the public, and it is always worth checking what is on.
Metro: Plaça d'Espanya. *Bus*: 100 (stop 10).

◆◆◆
SAGRADA FAMÍLIA
Plaça de la Sagrada Família
The Sagrada Família cathedral is the most amazing building in a city of extraordinary structures. It was the last and greatest work by Gaudí, who died (in 1926) before it was finished, and left Barcelona with a controversy which still rumbles on. Some people argue that it should be left incomplete, and that the unfinished building should become the centrepiece of a park dedicated to Antoni Gaudí. They feel there is no merit today in trying to guess the ideas of an architect who died some 65 years ago. For others completing the work is a passion, which ensures that bequests and donations continue to provide funds. Jordi Bonet Armengol, a son of one of Gaudí's collaborators, is the project's chief architect and believes that the undertaking will be fulfilled.
The cathedral's first architect was Francesc Villar, who conceived it as a neo-Gothic structure, on which work began in 1882. He partly completed the

crypt in which there is now a small museum. When Gaudí took charge soon after, he typically decided to do something completely different. There was to be a central tower rising to some 600 feet (180m) and three façades with other towers and spires dedicated to the Virgin, the Evangelists and Apostles. In his time only the Façana del Naixement (Nativity) facing Carrer de Marina, one of its four towers (Sant Barnabas) and the apse were completed. Now the Façana de la Pasiò (Passion), facing Carrer de Sardenya, and its towers are also complete and the entrance to the site is through this façade. Work is advancing on the third façade, Façana de la Gloria, facing Carrer Mallorca, which was originally to have been the main entrance. In the Façana del Naixement a lift goes up to a viewing platform from which there is a sweeping view of the cathedral site and the city beyond. No detailed plans were left by Gaudí, but his scale model (which was largely destroyed when anarchists attacked the building in 1935) has been painstakingly rebuilt. Apart from the cathedral's grandiose concept, the detail of the sculpture stays in the mind, and the way in which the whole structure conveys Christian symbolism. The integration of decoration into the flowing natural forms of the structure is another of the wonders of this building.

Craftspeople and artists such as the Japanese sculptor Etsuro Sotoo continue to interpret Gaudí's concepts. Not everyone likes the Temple Expiatori de la Sagrada Família (to give it its full name), but it never fails to impress one way or the other. You should not leave Barcelona without visiting and coming to your own conclusions about it. *Open*: summer 09.00–20.00hrs, winter 09.00–19.00hrs. *Metro*: Sagrada Família. *Bus*: 100 (stop 3).

Sagrada Família, Gaudí's apogee

◆◆◆
SANTA MARIA DEL MAR
Plaça Santa Maria
It took a relatively short time
(1329 to 1384) to built what is
one of the most beautiful of all
Catalan Gothic buildings. The
influential people of Barcelona
at that time wanted to celebrate
the city's wealth and power, and
did so by sponsoring the building
of this big new church. The
façade is very typical of the
place and period, with its strong
horizontal lines, big buttresses
and flat-topped octagonal
towers, but it is for its interior
that the church is most admired.
There is a tremendous feeling
of space, owing to the height of
the three naves and the
delicacy of the widely spaced
columns. The gloominess of
many churches is avoided too,
as the light filters through
beautiful stained glass windows
– the main rose window is

Stained glass, Santa Maria del Mar

especially fine. Concerts are
presented in the church.
Open: 08.00–13.00 and 17.00–
20.00hrs. *Metro*: Jaume 1.
Bus: 100 (stop 14).

◆◆
SANT GERVASI DISTRICT
Main draw for daytime visitors
to this barri is the upmarket
shopping in Avinguda Pau
Casals, in malls like Via Wagner
and in smaller streets where
there are also fashionable
eating and drinking places.
The Tramvia Blau tram moves
between the Tibidabo metro
station and the funicular to the
top of Tibidabo hill, with its
amusement park, wide views
and wooded areas.

◆
SANTS JUSTS I PASTOR
Plaça Sant Just
This Catalan Gothic church is
now fashionable for society
weddings. It was once the
parish church of Barcelona and
Aragón's count-kings, and is
believed by some to have been
built on the site of Barcelona's
first place of Christian worship.
Metro: Jaume I. *Bus*: 100 (stop
15).

◆
ZOO
Parc de la Ciutadella
The zoo has some 7,000 members
of around 500 species, from
killer whales to the tiniest
primates. Floc de Neu, the only
albino gorilla in captivity, steals
the show.
Open: summer 09.30–19.00hrs,
winter 10.00–17.00hrs. *Metro*:
Arc del Triomf, Barceloneta.
Bus: 100 (stop 14).

Walks in Barcelona

The outlines of three walks are suggested here. All of them are in interesting areas, with plenty of potential for detours and adaptations as you like. Without allowing for time spent visiting places of interest or for shopping and refreshments, each of the walks will take less than two hours. Places shown in **bold** type are more fully described in the preceding individual entries. The three walks all start at **Plaça de Catalunya**.

◆◆◆
WALK 1: LA RAMBLA

A few metres down on the right from Plaça de Catalunya is the **Font de Canaletes** which gives its name to this part of La Rambla. Groups gather around here for conversation, and people rent chairs to sit and watch the passing scene. The newspaper kiosks are open almost all the time and sell a wide selection from the foreign press. Note the Modernist decoration on the outside of the old pharmacy on the corner of Carrer Bonsuccés, and peep into the interior. Between this street and Carrer del Carme you are on the Rambla dels Estudis, named after a university which existed here until the early 18th century. Stalls sell a variety of caged birds, small animals and fish. Turn right down Carrer del Carme, past the 17th-century baroque façade of the Església de Betlem. You can go into the courtyards of the **Antic Hospital de la Santa Creu** on the left, and stroll through so that you come out on Carrer de

l'Hospital. Turn left, and when you reach La Rambla (here known as Rambla Sant Josep), turn left again. This section is also called the Rambla de les Flors because colourful flower stalls line the central walkway. The highlights of this stretch are the **Mercat de Sant Josep** and the **Palau de la Virreina**, both on your left. Cross La Rambla and note the neoclassical Palau Moja, headquarters of the Generalitat's Department of Culture and one of the remaining examples of fine palaces built during the 18th century. As you go into Carrer Portaferrissa, look out for the decorative fountain. This is the principal street for fashion shopping in the Ciutat Vella. Turn right into Carrer Petrixol, which is lined with art galleries and *granjes* serving delectable sweet goodies, coffee and chocolate. The street leads to the small Plaça del Pi, scene of an antiques market on Thursday, and of a 15th-century Gothic church with a magnificent rose window. Leave the plaça by walking through the shopping mall of Galeries Maldà. Back on Portaferrissa, go right to the Plaça Cucurulla where pavement artists are often at work. Turn right again down narrow Carrer del Pi to the attractive Plaça Sant Josep Oriol. An art and craft market is held here at weekends. Leave by the tiny Plaçeta del Pi on to Carrer Boqueria, and turn right towards the Plaça de Boqueria on La Rambla. Up on the right, a Chinese dragon decorates the Casa Bruno Quadras, by the Modernist architect Josep

Vilaseca. The umbrella motifs indicate that an umbrella shop originally occupied the ground floor. The ceramic tile decoration on La Rambla's central pavement was designed by Joan Miró. On the other side of La Rambla, note the Modernist exterior of the Antigua Casa Figueras. As you head on towards the sea you are on the Rambla dels Caputxins and the **Gran Teatre del Liceu** is on your right. In the warmer months the old-style Café de la Opera and other café bars operate along the centre. Go left into the **Plaça Reial** and when leaving it cross La Rambla to see Gaudí's **Palau Güell**. Back on La Rambla, turn right. The big Teatre Principal is on your right, and opposite on the Plaça del Teatre is the *Pitarra*, a Modernist memorial to Frederic Soler, who is regarded as the father of modern Catalan theatre. From here the last wide stretch is called Rambla Santa Mònica, which is the least salubrious part of La Rambla. On the righthand side is the **Centre d'Art Santa Mònica** and opposite is the Palau March, another survivor of the 18th-century palaces which once graced La Rambla. Down a passageway on the left is the Museu de Cera (wax museum – see under **Children**). La Rambla ends in the hopefully named Plaça Portal de la Pau (Gate of Peace) from which the **Monument a Colom** rises. Towards the right is the entrance to the **Museu Marítim**. From here you could continue left on to the **Moll de la Fusta**, for refreshments overlooking the harbour.

♦♦♦
WALK 2: THE BARRI GÒTIC
From the Plaça de Catalunya, start along La Rambla and then turn first left into Carrer de Santa Ana, a pedestrianised shopping street. Look out for the doorway on the left which leads to the pretty Plaçeta Ramon Amadeu. The Monestir de Santa Ana here, with its Romanesque church and Gothic cloister, is an unsung gem of Barcelona's architectural heritage. Leave the same way and take the tiny lane opposite into Plaça Villa de Madrid. On the corner to your right is the Ateneu Barcelonès, a cultural institution which holds good exhibitions in its 18th-century building. Go past the Hotel Villa Madrid, turn left into the small lane, and then right to reach Plaça Cucurulla, then turn into Carrer Boters to reach Plaça Nova. Picasso designed the mural for the modern Institute of Architects building on the left. Ahead is the Portal del Bisbe, whose two round towers, later modified, were built as part of the Roman wall. Just through the portal here is the Palau del Bisbe (Episcopal Palace), whose fine 12th-century courtyard can be spied through the gate. In the lane on your left, look into the attractive patio of the Casa de l'Ardiaca (Archdeacon's House) with its beautiful Gothic fountain. The house is a 15th-century reconstruction of an earlier building, and now houses the Institute of Municipal History. Opposite is the Romanesque chapel of Santa Llúcia, which has a doorway into the cathedral cloister. Back in the

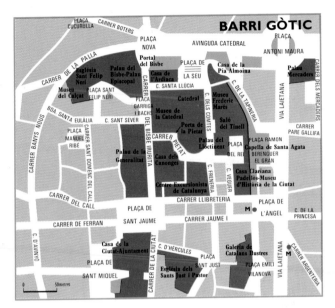

Carrer del Bisbe, go left into a small square, where it is quite likely there will be buskers performing. Go right down the side of the Palau del Bisbe and note the very old frescos on its façade. An arch leads you into one of the city's most beguiling corners, the Plaça Sant Felip Neri. Concerts are held in the church on the right. Here too is the odd little Museu del Calçat (shoe museum – *open*: Tuesday to Saturday 11.00–14.00hrs). Leave the plaça by the opposite exit and turn left to get back to Carrer del Bisbe. The Casa dels Canonges (Canons' House) on the right was built in the 14th century but has been much changed. On the left the Porta de la Pietat (Door of Pity) leads into the cathedral cloister. The door gets its name from the

wooden relief above the entrance. Continue around to the right to reach the doorway to the Centre Excursionista de Catalunya, an influential association of lovers of the Catalan landscape. Inside, columns from the Roman temple of Augustus can be seen. When you reach the Plaça de Sant Jaume, where the buildings of the **Generalitat** and Ajuntament (**Casa de la Ciutat**) face each other, go down the left side of the Ajuntament, noting its original façade. Take the first left to reach Plaça Sant Just, which is dominated by the church of **Sants Just i Pastor**. The fountain dates from the 14th century. Down Carrer Bisbe Caçador, the handsome Palau de Comtessa de Palamós now houses the Galeria de Catalans

Ilustres (Academy of Literature and Illustrious Catalans). Leave Plaça Sant Just via Carrer de Lledò, which has examples of the grand houses built by the business community during the city's medieval heyday. Cross Carrer Jaume I, then go first right and first left. You will already have seen quite a few interesting shops on this walk, and there are more in this vicinity. The **Museu d'Història de la Ciutat** is on the right, followed by the captivating ensemble of the **Plaça del Rei**. Leave it by bearing right, and with the mass of the cathedral on your left, you should reach the **Museu Frederic Marés**. From the Plaça de la Seu you can admire the impressive façade of the **Catedral**. As you look down the steps, the building on the right is the Casa Pia Almoina, mainly 15th-century, which housed a charitable institution committed to feeding 100 people each day. Go around it to the right, and follow the remains of the Roman wall to the Plaça Ramon Berenguer el Gran, where an equestrian statue by Josep Llimona commemorates Ramon Berenguer III, Count of Barcelona. There are five well-restored towers and curtain walls from the Roman fortifications here.

If you have had enough walking, you can return to Plaça de l'Angel and join the metro from Jaume I to go elsewhere. To continue the walk, go left into Carrer Salvador Aulet, across Via Laietana into Carrer Manresa, and right into Carrer Argenteria (Plateria) to the grand church of **Santa Maria del Mar**. Go along the side of the church into Passeig del Born, making sorties into side streets which have art galleries and craft shops. The big wrought-iron building of the Mercat del Born, now used for rallies and fairs, was completed in 1876 by architects Mestres and Fontseré. They were also responsible for the completion of the cathedral's main façade. Back near the church, go right into the Plaçeta and Carrer Montcada which is lined by fine palaces. This is one of the most popular tourist streets in the city because the **Museu Picasso** is located at its upper end. It also has the **Museu Tèxtil i de la Indumentària** and interesting art galleries and shops.

◆◆◆
WALK 3: THE EIXAMPLE

Leave the Plaça de Catalunya on the northwest corner into Passeig de Gràcia and go first right into Carrer de Casp. The Renaissance-inspired touches on the façade of number 46 are by one of the lesser-known Modernist architects, Juli Batllevell. On the corner with Carrer del Bruc, you can see the Casa Calvet, which Gaudí completed in 1900. It shows baroque influences in its decoration. Turn left up Carrer del Bruc crossing Gran Via de les Corts Catalanes and two more streets to reach Carrer d'Aragó. Look out for examples of less publicised Modernist works on the way. (Over to the left on Carrer Aragó is one of the oldest buildings in the Eixample, the 15th-century

Església de la Concepció which has an attractive cloister.) Cross to the right over Carrer Aragó and cross the **Mercat Concepció** to the opposite exit. Go left along Carrer València and before turning right into Carrer Roger de Lluria notice on your left the Modernist Conservatori Municipal de Música, completed by Antoni de Falguera in 1914. On the left corner of Carrers Roger de Lluria and Mallorca is the Palau Montaner, by Domènech i Montaner. Domènech also designed Casa Thomas, to the right at Mallorca 291, which now houses the design store, B D Ediciones. Continue along Roger de Lluria to Avinguda Diagonal. Across to the left is the big triangular block of the Casa Terrades (Casa de les Punxes) designed by Puig i Cadalfach. Turn left and one block on is his Casa Quadras which houses the **Museu de la Música**. Almost opposite is the flowery front of the Casa Comalat by Modernist architect Salvador Valeri i Pupurull. Go left into Passeig de Gràcia: from now on the many elegant shops will no doubt draw you to their well-dressed windows. The decorative streetlamps and benches are by the Modernist Pere de Falquès. Gaudí's **Casa Mila** dominates the second block on the left. Further down, on the opposite side between Carrers de València and d'Aragó, are the Bulevar Rosa, Centre de Anticuaris and Centre Permanent d'Artesania (see **Shopping**). The next block is the Manzana de Discordia, or Block of Discord, with the **Casa Amatller, Casa Batlló** and **Casa Lleó-Morera**. Go right along Carrer Consell de Cent, which has several art galleries, and right into Carrer de Balmes. First right and opposite is the **Fundació Tàpies**. Turn right and walk back to the Plaça de Catalunya along the pleasant central walkway of Rambla de Catalunya.

Plaça de Catalunya is the city's hub

Excursions from Barcelona

Catalunya is not a very large region, but it has a lot of variety and many areas of great natural beauty. It is also packed with places of historic interest, including some very attractive spots. As distances are relatively short, Barcelona is a convenient base from which to make day excursions. Both the road and rail systems are good and there are organised coach excursions to quite a few places. Renfe, the national rail company, and FGC, the Generalitat's rail network, have restored old rolling stock and locomotives (some of them steam powered), and operate special tourist trains to a few destinations.

This is a small sample of the many places worth a visit. Opening times and public transport services are subject to change and are also affected by local holidays, so it is always wise to get the latest information from the Generalitat's tourist office at Gran Via de les Corts Catalanes 658 before planning an excursion.

◆◆◆
MONTSERRAT

30 miles (48km) west of Barcelona

Montserrat is a mass of sandstone and conglomerate rock with a serrated spine rising to some 4,000 feet (1,220m) above the plain. It can be seen from far away, and makes an impressive natural feature, but it is a small dark statue and its legend which gives the mountain its great significance. Montserrat is the spiritual centre

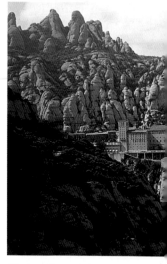

Montserrat's mountain monastery

of the Catalan people, with a monastery and a basilica, completed in 1592. The basilica is the home of the image of La Mare de Deu (The Mother of God), blackened by the smoke of millions of candles over the centuries and affectionately known as La Morenita (The Dark One). She is said to have been made by St Luke and brought to the area by St Peter. When the Moors invaded in the 8th century she was hidden in what is now called the Santa Cova (Holy Cave) and when discovered there in AD880 she refused to be moved. A shrine and chapel were built and nuns guarded her until AD976, when a Benedictine monastery was first established. It became an influential centre of learning and culture, and many notables visited it to pay their respects to

the Virgin. Napoleon's army sacked the monastery in 1811 and it sank into decline until 1874 when monks returned and began rebuilding it. The monastery buildings look more suited to an army but they provide the 300 monks, and their visitors, with modern comforts: there are hostels, restaurants and shops. Paintings and sculpture adorn the basilica and are displayed in the museum, and at 13.00hrs (except in July) a boys' choir, known as La Escolania, sings in the basilica.

Hermitages dot the mountain-side and there are many paths to walk, with views far and wide (you can sometimes see as far as Mallorca). It is an hour's walk or a short funicular ride to Sant Jeromi hermitage, which stands near the highest point of the mountain.

Montserrat is clearly signposted for drivers from Barcelona. Take the A2/A7 (E4) autopista (direction Lleida and Tarragona), and join the N11 at exit 25, then follow local road C1411 and a twisting scenic drive up the mountain. Or take the train — the FGC service from Plaça d'Espanya — and then the cable car. Enquire at the station about the *Cami de Montserrat*, a combined ticket for train, cable car and funiculars.

◆◆
SITGES
26 miles (42km) south

Sitges is an old grandee among Spain's resorts — it is one of those which defies the claim that all Spanish resorts are ugly ribbons of concrete high-rises along the seashore. It remains elegant, despite some signs of wear and neglect — somehow these only add to the general charm. Sitges has for a long time been the weekend and holiday playground of Barcelonans, and the smart villas of wealthy families along the Passeig Marítim and in the areas of Vinyet and Terramar include examples of Modernist and *noucentiste* architecture. It has had a reputation for being favoured by creative people since the versatile Modernist Santiago Rusinyol first brought the town to the attention of the artistic community with his Festes Modernistes which he started in 1892. His home, Cau Ferrat, became the meeting place for leading artists of the period. Today it is an interesting museum which contains two paintings by El Greco. Next door is the Museu Maricel, beside the picturesque 17th-century parish church on the promontory, which is the most attractive part of the town. Near Carrer Parellades (the main shopping street), the Museu Romàntic in the Casa Llopis displays the furniture and effects of a wealthy 19th-century home. North of the promontory is the smaller beach of Platja de Sant Sebastia, and beyond that lie the sports marina and modern residential development of Aiguadolc. A palm-fringed promenade runs beside the long, wide and well-maintained beach to the south. In February, Sitges shakes off any winter blues it may have and bursts into the festivities and parades of its colourful Carnival, which draws people from afar. It is also known for its enthusiastic celebration of Corpus Christi, (in June) when streets are carpeted with bright flowers, and in May it hosts an exhibition of carnations, Spain's national flower. Throughout the year, (though less so in the summer), there are festivals of music, dance and theatre. The tourist office (tel: 894 4700) is behind the Oasis shopping centre, near the market and Renfe station. To get there by road from Barcelona, take the C246 autovia past the airport and through the resort of Castelldefels, from which there is a scenic corniche road of 12 miles (19km). An alternative fast toll road is being cut though the Garraf mountain. See also **Vilafranca del Penedés and Sant Sadurní**, which could be taken in on a visit to Sitges.

Regular Renfe train services run along the coast from Passeig de Gràcia and Central-Sants stations, and take less than 45 minutes.

◆◆
VILAFRANCA DEL PENEDÉS AND SANT SADURNÍ DE ANOIA

22 miles (35km) southwest
Vilafranca is the main town of the Penedés wine producing region. It has some picturesque corners to discover but the main attractions are its unusually good small museum, which is housed in a 14th-century palace of the kings of Aragón, and a visit to the Torres bodega. The Museu de Vi chronicles winemaking since ancient times, and on the top floor there is a well-arranged display of the region's bird life. Vilafranca is well known for its *castellers* – acrobats who build tall human pyramids and can often be seen doing so at weekends in the plaça named after them. Most producers of the champagne method *cava* wines have their headquarters in the nearby town of Sant Sadurní; the two big producers, Freixenet and Cordoniú, offer entertaining and educational tours lasting around one and a half hours. Both Vilafranca and Sant Sadurní have numerous restaurants, where good regional dishes are accompanied by fine wines and cavas.
The main road from Barcelona is autopista A2/A7 (E4) (direction Lleida and Tarragona): take exit 27. There are Renfe rail services from Central-Sants station.

PEACE AND QUIET

Wildlife and Countryside in and around Barcelona
by Paul Sterry

Although many of the beaches and shores north and south of Barcelona have been developed for tourism and have lost their wildlife appeal, there are still large tracts of rugged, wooded coastline left. Travel inland and you will find even more variety: high sierras, arid semi-deserts and the Pyrenees.

The Coast

It is ironic that the development necessary to accommodate tens of thousands of tourists has led to many of the best beaches and wetland habitats being spoilt both in appearance and for wildlife. However, the steep cliffs survive, more or less unspoilt, and wherever you go along the coast there will be something of interest.

> **Gulls**
> Although comparatively few and far between, any gulls you might see are worth studying closely. The yellow-legged race of herring gull will be most numerous, but look out for Mediterranean gulls, which have pure white wings, a black hood in summer and a loud 'cow-cow-cow' call. Audouin's gulls are sometimes seen; they have comparatively slender wings and a thin bill and always lack a dark hood. This is one of the rarest gulls in the world and is only found in the Mediterranean.

Rocky outcrops may be cloaked in colourful native flowers and the introduced Hottentot fig, which tumbles in anarchic jumbles of waxy green leaves and red flowers.

Costa Brava – the Spanish name means Wild Coast

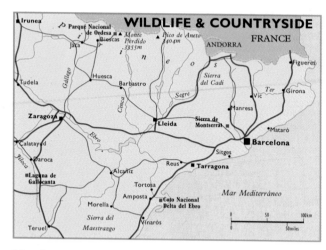

WILDLIFE & COUNTRYSIDE

Maquis

Maquis is the name given to the fragrant, tangled vegetation covering many hillsides along the Catalan coast. The scent of rosemary, thyme and lavender pervades the air, and from March until June a dazzling array of colourful flowers is in bloom.

Shrubs and trees such as kermes oak, strawberry tree and olive are often found, but the true delight of the maquis lies nearer the ground. Several species of cistus can be found (each with papery flowers and waxy or aromatic leaves), along with tree heathers, species of broom and gorse, and orchids. Insects abound in the maquis: colourful butterflies, day-flying hummingbird hawk moths and shiny rose chafer beetles move from flower to flower in search of nectar. Although the maquis scrub may be largely impenetrable, birdwatchers should not despair. Stand still for long enough and you should see and hear species such as hoopoes — large birds with orange and black plumage and a floppy flight pattern — or Sardinian warblers, small, dark birds with black heads and very distinctive red eye rings.

Woodland

Compared to much of the Mediterranean, Catalunya still possesses large areas of woodland. Along the coast this is largely made up of aleppo pines, stone pines and cork oaks. Inland, beyond the ridge of hills that border the coast, woods of sweet chestnut can be found.

Along glades and paths among the coastal woods, a rich flora often develops which has many species in common with areas of maquis. Brooms, gorses and tree heathers are conspicuous, with other species such as cistuses, orchids and lavenders adding splashes of colour. The birdlife of these woodlands is also often similar to that found in maquis. However, in undisturbed areas look and listen for golden orioles – the song is loud and fluty, the bird an astonishing sun-yellow. After dark, you may be lucky enough to hear a Scop's owl, the call of which is a repetitive sonar-like bleep, quite unlike any other bird's call.

Spring Flowers

Although the Barcelona region receives more rainfall (700–800mm per annum) than areas further south on the Spanish coast, there is still a distinct dry season from June to October. During this period, much of the vegetation becomes parched and lifeless, and visitors could be forgiven for assuming that little grows here at all. Return in late winter or early spring and it is quite a different matter: plant life burgeons and colourful flowers greet the eye.

Although some of the flowers are evergreen and can withstand the summer drought, others survive as underground bulbs and tubers. After the first autumn rains, leaves appear and they begin to grow, with many species flowering during the early spring. Among the more characteristic species to bloom in spring are poppies, crocuses, vetches, squills, grape hyacinths and irises. Wild orchids can also be found in abundance in many parts of the Catalan countryside. Members of the bee orchid family are widespread – yellow bee, mirror and bumblebee being among them – as well as man orchids and butterfly orchids, their names reflecting their curious appearances. One of the most striking and beautiful species is the violet limodore, which produces tall spikes of deep purple flowers in shady woodland.

Cistus thrives in the maquis

PEACE AND QUIET

Sierra de Montserrat

The Mare de Deu image in the
monastery here draws many
visitors. The monastery's setting,
amid towering pillars of rock, is
imposing in itself, but the plants
and birds of the area also have
much to offer anyone with an
interest in natural history.
Montserrat is 30 miles (48km)
from Barcelona. Take the N11
road towards Lleida and then
turn off to Monistrol on the local
road C1411.

The Ebro Delta

The vast Ebro Delta empties
into the Mediterranean near
Tortosa. It is a region of
wetlands and rice paddies —
home to thousands of wintering
and breeding birds. Although
much of the delta is agricultural,
some of the best areas are now
protected as the Coto Nacional
Delta del Ebro. From the main
A7 road take the 340 to
Amposta. One road to the north

Rock bunting

Birds of Montserrat
*Among the oak and pine
woodland and maquis look for
these birds:*
Sardinian warbler
Hoopoe
Bee-eater
Serin
Woodchat shrike

Higher up look for:
Blue rock thrush
Rock sparrow
Rock bunting
Crag martin
Alpine swift

In the sky:
Booted eagle
Short-toed eagle
Buzzard
Griffon vulture

---

of the village runs north of the
river; another to the south of the
village allows exploration of the
southern half of the delta.
The flooded fields, lagoons and
drainage canals are among the
easiest areas to watch birds,

The semi-desert of Zaragoza

with minor roads and tracks throughout. The 'zip-zip-zip' song of fan-tailed warblers can be heard almost everywhere, and egrets and spoonbills are regularly seen. Flamingos are also often present. Black-winged stilts, resplendent with their black-and-white plumage and incredibly long, red legs, probe the margins for food, and avocets scythe the water with upturned bills.

Reedbeds are not the easiest of habitats to observe, but those in the Ebro Delta are worth persevering with to discover some of their more interesting birds. Warblers advertise their territories with song, and purple herons and little bitterns skulk secretively through the vegetation. Sometimes these birds are startled into flight if a bird of prey passes overhead.

Zaragoza

Inland from the mountains that fringe Spain's Mediterranean coast lie many dry regions with the appearance of semi-desert. Although parts of Zaragoza are now agricultural, there are still large tracts of arid land that are home to some of fhe country's most unusual birds.

Birds of Zaragoza

Larks, more than any other group of small birds, find the semi-deserts of the province much to their liking. Short-toed, Calandra and crested larks are widespread, but in a few unspoilt areas, Thekla and Dupont's lark occur. The latter is really a North African species, but has isolated outposts in northern Spain. Other birds to look for include pin-tailed and black-bellied sandgrouse, stone curlews, little bustards and great grey shrikes. Griffon vultures are ever-present in the skies above. They breed, together with a few pairs of Egyptian vultures, in some of the sandstone gorges carved by rivers in the province.

PEACE AND QUIET

Set amid these arid lands is an oasis of water. The Laguna de Gallocanta is a national refuge and is a sanctuary for vast numbers of birds. In the winter months, large flocks of cranes arrive, together with thousands of wildfowl and coots. Herons and egrets are abundant and black-winged stilts are one of the most conspicuous waders around the shoreline. The lake is distinctly saline, and has plants more usually associated with the seashore than an inland lake. Laguna de Gallocanta is Spain's largest natural inland lake. To reach it, drive to Calatayud, take the N234 southeast to Daroca and the C211 west. The lake shore can be explored along minor roads and tracks running through the surrounding area.

Ordesa National Park

The Pyrenees

If you have a few days to spare, a trip to the Pyrenees provides a complete contrast to the Mediterranean coast around Barcelona. For those on a short stay, the Parque Nacional de Ordesa (Ordesa National Park) is probably the best area to visit. From the comparatively low-lying valleys, full of splendid wild flowers, those with energy to spare can walk high into the mountains. Here visitors will find specialised mountain flowers, many of which are endemic to the Pyrenees, along with chamois and exciting birds such as lammergeiers, wallcreepers and citril finches. To reach the park entrance at Ordesa, drive to Huesca, then take the C136 north to Biescas and head east along the C140 to Tovla. From here the entrance is signposted.

FOOD AND DRINK

Catalunya ranks with the Basque country as the best regions in Spain for good food. It also scores high marks for its fine wines. Visitors to Barcelona have no reason to complain about the general standards in the quality of food, its preparation, the choices available, or the range of places in which to enjoy it. The main drawback, which Barcelonans themselves increasingly complain about, is the rising cost of eating and drinking out. The problem is relative however − costs of meals are on a par with those in other West European cities, less in the most basic eating places. Alcoholic drinks are cheaper: sometimes they may seem to cost the same, but the measures will be larger.

As elsewhere in Spain, many bars sell tapas (small, tasty snacks) and *raciones* (larger portions).

There are distinct variations in cuisine between different parts of Catalunya. Barcelona itself has traditionally had two cooking styles, that of the bourgeoisie (much influenced by France) and the more filling dishes of peasant origin cooked by the working people. As the regional capital, it has adopted cooking styles from the rest of Catalunya, and in recent times innovative chefs have adapted traditional recipes to make lighter dishes, to satisfy modern tastes and dietary concerns. Catalans share the Mediterranean custom of liberally using olive oil, but traditionally they also used lard more than other Spaniards. Now cooking in fats is less frequent, and there is a preference for steaming. Heavy seasoning of sauces is avoided, with good use made of the food's own juices, and garlic is used with greater discretion.

Catalunya has the advantage of being able to harvest an abundance and a wide variety of foods from both land and sea. The cooking is distinguished by unexpected and subtle combinations of tastes and products, such as pears with duck or chicken with lobster. Although throughout the year many of the same ingredients are used and some dishes remain almost daily favourites, you will also find seasonal variations, reflecting a habit of preparing whatever is best at the time. These are some of the things to look out for in the different seasons: spring − lamb, kid and sprouting vegetables; summer − fish, salads, rice dishes and fruit; autumn − game, mushrooms, dried fruit, nuts; winter − broths (like the staple *escudella*), the Barcelonan speciality of monkfish soup, cabbage and cauliflower, legumes and citrus fruit. Cod (*bacallà*) is the most widely used fish. Pork (*porc*) is the staple meat and flavours the cooking of other foods. Lamb (*xai*) is especially good in Catalunya, and so are the region's many different sausages and cooked meats. Pastries are eaten as breakfast or with coffee and chocolate throughout the day, and different pastries are associated with different annual festivities. There are five basic sauces in Catalunyan cooking. *Sofregit* is a cooked blend of oil, onion, garlic and tomato; *samfaina* is made by adding chopped sweet pepper, courgette and aubergine to this. Almonds, filberts, garlic, parsley, and sometimes fried bread, are pounded in a mortar to blend into a *picada* sauce. Chefs maintain great secrecy about recipes for their *romesco* sauces, of which almonds are the base. Olive oil and garlic are blended to make *allioli* which can in turn be blended into mayonnaise. Hot spices are not much used for seasoning and the preference is for aromatic herbs: fennel, bay leaves and parsley for fish; thyme for meat; juniper berries with game; mint with broad beans and other vegetables.

A feast from land and sea

Cinnamon flavours some pastas and broths; saffron is used in a variety of dishes; chocolate is added to colour stews and game dishes. One of the delights of Catalan cuisine is the variety of fresh vegetables and the way the flavours of the cooked foods' juices are widely used as seasoning.

Restaurants catering for the tourist trade have menu translations, but if you want to try other places it helps to know the names of some standby dishes. Eaten at any time of the day, by itself or as an accompaniment, is a *pa amb tomaquet*, bread rubbed with tomato and garlic and seasoned with olive oil and salt. *Escalivada* is a cooked salad of peppers and aubergines, while *esqueixada* is a raw salad of salted cod, peppers and onions. *Espinacs a la Catalana* is spinach with raisins and pine nuts. Pastas are popular and *canelons* (canelloni) appear on many menus. *Fideus* is much like the better known rice-and-seafood *paella*, but noodles are used instead of rice. In *arros negre*, rice is cooked in the ink of squid. Fish stews are usually very good, and are known as *suquets*. *Escudella i carn d'olla* is a meat and vegetable stew served as two courses. The broth, *escudella,* is served first with rice or *galets*, a broad pasta, and *pilotas*, spongy meat balls flavoured with parsley, garlic, cinnamon and pine nuts. This is followed by the boiled meats, the *carn d'olla*. For dessert there is *crema catalana*, a caramel cream dessert also popular elsewhere in Spain.

Eating Times and Places

The day starts with a simple breakfast of coffee and a croissant or some *pastises* (pastries) — widely available in cafés and bars. By the middle of the morning you might be ready for a sandwich — again, they are sold at bars and cafés. After an *aperitivo*, lunch starts around 14.00hrs and, as the main meal of the day, goes on until around 16.00hrs. Between 18.00 and 19.00hrs locals have a *merienda*, when pastries are eaten with coffee or a chocolate drink. At home the evening meal is something light around 22.00hrs. This is also the best time to try for dinner at a restaurant. Restaurants often offer a *menú del día* (fixed price menu) at lunchtime. In basic eateries this can be fair value for filling food. In more sophisticated places it is often an unsatisfactory

Patriotic colours for puddings

compromise, and you can do better by choosing well from the *carta* (menu). Many restaurants are closed on Sunday evenings and on Mondays, and some restaurants close in August for their annual holidays. Besides restaurants, there are many other places where you can get something to eat: takeaways; cafeterias; international franchise operations; bars which serve tapas (snacks); and *granjes*, which are milk bars. Or you can go to a market, *xarcuteria* (cooked meat shop) and *forn de pan* (bakery), to buy ingredients for a delectable outdoor lunch in one of the city's delightful open spaces.

Wines

You can have an enjoyable time in Barcelona getting to know the wines of Catalunya, which has eight *Denominaciones de Origen*, or DOs, which are controlled wine producing areas. This is the second largest wine producer among Spain's regions. The best known and largest volume DO area is Penedés within Barcelona province. The family firm of Torres is the leading producer and most successful exporter. Penedés whites are drunk young, when they are light and fruity; rosés are much the same but slightly more vigorous. Reds are also generally light and the best of them, such as Torres Gran Coronas, are well rounded and velvety. Alella, along the Costa Maresme, is the other DO area in Barcelona province, and produces good whites, both dry and sweet. Catalunya's other provinces have DO areas of their own. Priorat in Tarragona province produces rich, strong reds and sweet dessert wines; other DOs in this province are Tarragona, Terra Alta (a variety of wines but in small volumes), and Conca de Barberà, which is growing in importance as a producer of whites and rosés. Girona province has Empordà-Costa Brava, especially known for its rosés, and Perelada's Blanc Pescador, a light, sparkling white. Lleida province offers Costers del Segre, with young white and mature, mellow reds, which are good but not yet widely appreciated. The town of Sant Sadurní d'Anoia in the Penedés area is the centre of production of Catalunya's *cava* — sparkling wine made by the champagne method. Cava has been very successful in the international market and the two leading producers, Freixenet and Cordoniú, outsell French champagne in the United States. The best quality cava is *brut* and *brut nature*.

Other Drinks

Tap water is usually safe, but to be on the safe side drink bottled water, *agua mineral*. Coffee is a very popular drink, and is served in various sizes and strengths, often laced with brandy. With milk it is *café amb llet*. Rich creamy chocolate is drunk in the morning, for *merienda* and as a nightcap. *Manzanilla* is an infusion of camomile, credited with calming properties. Ordinary Spanish beer has more than 5 per cent alcohol per volume, which means it is stronger than

ordinary beer in most European countries. *Una caña* (from the tap) is usually cheaper than bottled beer. Catalunya produces good brandies and again Torres is a leading mark: try a Torres Diez Reserva. There is also a wide choice of liqueurs and the full range of imported spirits and beers.

Where to Eat

Finding places to eat well in every price category is not difficult in Barcelona — the biggest problem is choosing from the vast range available. It is not unknown for visitors to be so bemused by the choice that they end up in a hamburger joint or some other mediocre place. The following list of restaurants is by no means exhaustive, and there are very many more which could be included. As well as suggesting specific places, the list leads you into areas and streets where there are other eateries, and gives an idea of the sort of places you can find in the city. The emphasis is on places with moderate prices where you can expect to pay between 3,000 and 5,000 pesetas per person for a three-course meal. Restaurants are first shown under city districts and then briefly described in the listing by type of cuisine. Besides these districts, remember the Poble Espanyol on Montjuïc has a choice of eating places.

In the Ciutat Vella

There are many tourist traps here, but you will also find unassuming, family-run eateries serving filling fare to local people. These are usually best at lunchtime and include: **La Cassola**, Sant Sever 3, in the Barri Gòtic; **Quatre Barres**, Quintana 6, off Carrer de Ferran and near La Rambla (smarter and pricier); **Egipte**, Jerusalem 12, behind Mercat de Sant Josep; and **Rodrigo** in Argenteria off Via Laietana. **Vegetariano**, Canuda 41, is good for vegetable and salad dishes (no alcohol or smoking). See listings by type of cuisine for: **Agu d'Avignon**, d'Avinyo/La Trinitat; **Blau Mari**, Moll de la Fusta 1; **Café de l'Academia**, de Lladó 1; **Can Majó**, Almirante Aixade 23 (Barceloneta); **Los Caracoles**, Escudellers 14; **La Perla Nera**, Via Laietana 32–4; **Senyor Parellada**, Argenteria 37; **Shalimar**, Carmen 71; and **Els Quatre Gats**, Montsió 3.

In the Eixample
Several places have a good value *menú del día* (fixed price menu for the day) to satisfy their regular lunchtime customers. It is a good idea to scour around looking at menus displayed outside. See listings by type of cuisine for: **Alt Heidelberg**, Ronda Universitat 5; **Café de Londres**, Londres 103; **Chino Long Hua**, Passatge Marimón 6; **La Manduca**, Girona 59; **Mordisco**, Rosselló 265; **L'Olive**, Muntaner 171; **Els Perols de l'Empordà**, Villarroel 88; **Petit President**, Passatge Marimón 20; **Los Ponchos**, València 196; and **Yamadory-Japones**, Aribau 68.

In Sarria-Sant Gervasi
Places like **La Cova del Drac**, Tuset 30 (better known as a nighttime jazz venue) and **Can Tripas**, Saguès 16, are lively and serve basic fare at lunchtime.

Follow the signs to Els Quatre Gats

Taita, Maestre Nicolau 9, is trendy, a bit pricier and has a pretty terrace. See listings by type of cuisine for: **El Cus-Cus**, Plaça Cardona 4; **El Dorado Petit**, Dolors Monserdà 51; **Flash-Flash**, La Granada del Penedés 25; **Henry J Bean's**, La Granada 14; **Network**, Diagonal 616; **Patxi**, Bonavista 21; and **Shahenshah**, Vallmajor 33.

American
Henry J Bean's, La Granada 14 (tel: 218 2998). Chicago sets the tone for decór and dishes — hamburgers, ribs and salads. The other 'my kinda town' place, **The Chicago Pizza Pie Factory**, Provença 300, specialises in deep dish pizzas. Both are cheap and cheerful.

FOOD AND DRINK

Basque

Patxi, Bonavista 21 (tel: 217 2157). This is a good place to try classic Basque dishes like *merluza a la vasca* (hake) at reasonable prices. The lunchtime *menú del día* is very good value.

Catalan

Agut d'Avignon, D'Avinyo/La Trinitat (tel: 302 6034). A traditional place with a famed cellar, Agut d'Avignon is a favourite lunchtime haunt of the city's art critics and is much used by officials from the nearby Generalitat and Ajuntament. Specialities include regional dishes like partridge with grapes, rabbit with almonds and fish with *romesco* sauce. Prices are on the upper side of moderate.

Café de l'Academia, de Lladó 1 (tel: 315 0026). Rustic decor, classical music, delectable dishes and honest prices win hearts here. It is run by a charming and professional

Feast the eye at Los Caracoles

couple with an all-female kitchen team who prepare traditional favourites and modern variations. In the mornings, there are very tasty sandwiches. Understandably very popular – you may have difficulty getting a table at lunchtime.

Can Majó, Almirante Aixade 23 (Barceloneta) (tel: 310 5096). The smartest seafood restaurant in an area which has many similar establishments. Follow the chef's seasonal recommendations, which may include *centollos*, delicious crabs from the north coast. The *suquet de peix* (bouillabaisse) is delicious. Dishes based on rice are among other specialities. Prices are on the high side of moderate.

Can Travi Nou, Antic Cami de Sand Cebrià (to the northwest of the centre, in Horta-Guinardó) (tel: 428 0301). An 18th-century *masia* (mansion) beyond the city centre. Its conversion into a restaurant eight years ago was faithful to the period, and it has become one of the city's top

restaurants. In summer you can eat outside on the terrace. Most of chef Josep Mercader's menu is Catalan, both traditional and modern, but with international touches. The wine list extends to 500 wines and cavas. Prices are reasonable by international standards for this sort of quality.
Los Caracoles, Escudellers 14 (tel: 302 3185). Go here at lunchtime rather than at night, when the area is a bit rough. The way in is through the kitchen. You will no doubt see many tourists at the tables but that does nothing to diminish the character of this genuine and bustling Barcelonan eatery, which offers good cooking of Catalan and other regional specialities. If you just want something cheap and/or simple, the grilled chicken is a good choice. Other prices are moderate.
El Dorado Petit, Dolors Monserdà 51 (tel: 204 5506). Lluis Cruañas has created what is widely rated as one of Spain's top restaurants, in a suburban villa above the city. You can dine in elegance indoors, or outside on the pretty terrace in summer. Presentation and service are impeccable. Traditional recipes of the Gironan districts of Empordà inspire the *nouvelle* preparation of the best and freshest ingredients. If the choice is too agonising, try the *menú de degustación* which provides delectable, and quite filling, tastes of the house specialities. You will probably not see any change out of 12,000 pesetas per person including drinks.
La Manduca, Girona 59 (tel: 302

3137). The ebullient owner and rustic decoration create a welcoming, homely atmosphere, and his son and the other waiters give friendly, attentive service. The cooking is mainly traditional Catalan, and prices are moderate.
Mordisco, Rosselló 265 (tel: 218 3314). Simple but imaginative combinations of high quality ingredients are served here in a pleasant setting, which includes works of modern art. Try a selection from the salad bar, or go for one of the daily special dishes – they may sound strange but are well worth a try. Open from 08.30 to 02.00hrs, except Sundays, Mordisco is fashionable and always busy, with budget prices.
L'Olive, Muntaner 171 (tel: 230 9027). A first rate, busy brasserie with fast, efficient service. The *cuina de mercat* menu offers fresh seasonal produce and fish, prepared with flair. Prices are moderate.
Els Perols de l'Empordà, Villarroel 88 (tel: 323 1033). Rinaldo Serrat and Julieta Fausellas run a quiet restaurant where the cooking is faithful to its origin and prices are reasonable. The Empordà area of Girona province is known for its tasty combinations of produce from land and sea, and here they excel at them, in dishes like *pollastre amb llagostins* (chicken and lobster) and *arros negre*.
Els Quatre Gats, Montsió 3 (tel: 302 4140). The original Els Quatre Gats Café was where artists gathered in the early 1900s, including the young Picasso. It became a dress shop

FOOD AND DRINK

in 1936 but was revived as a café restaurant in 1983 by Pere Notó and Ricard Alsina. The setting is the Modernist Casa Martí building by Puig i Cadalfach. There is art on the walls, and exhibitions are held here; you can also hear live music. Catalan dishes predominate on a menu which is relatively expensive.

Senyor Parellada, Argenteria 37 (tel: 315 4010). Ramón Parellada's family owns one of Catalunya's oldest hostelries, the Fonda Europa in Granollers, and he has transplanted much of its ambience to Barcelona. The innovative and amusingly named dishes are mostly inspired by Catalan and French cuisine. It is wise to listen to Senyor Parellada or his maitre d's advice as to what is best from the market that day. Service is very attentive, but the tables are sometimes too close together for the comfort of waiters or customers. Good value.

Eastern

Chino Long Hua, Passatge Marimón 6 (tel: 201 8713). Unpretentious, cheap and fairly faithful to the most popular of Cantonese recipes.

Shahenshah, Vallmajor 33 (tel: 209 0927). The decoration and furnishings are in authentic northern Indian style, and equal care is taken to be faithful to traditional Hindu cooking of the region. The main concession to local palates is a lighter touch with strong spices. Prices are moderate: not very cheap, but not *very* expensive either.

Shalimar, Carmen 71 (tel: 329

3496). Pakistani Muslim dishes with *halal* meat specialities: cheap, with takeaway service.

Yamadory-Japones, Aribau 68 (tel: 253 9264). One of Barcelona's first Japanese restaurants, it still ranks among the best. An inscrutable chef prepares a variety of raw fish dishes at the *sushi* bar, and there is also a good choice of delicately prepared cooked dishes. Private rooms are available for dining in traditional style. Its sister restaurant,

Yashima, Josep Tarradellas 145 (tel: 419 0697), offers a *menú de degustación* of eight dishes. Both places are moderately priced, given their high standards.

German

Alt Heidelberg, Ronda Universitat 5 (tel: 302 1037). Over 50 years the *cervecería* (bar) and restaurant has been a great favourite for its wide selection of beers, tasty sandwiches, interesting salads and hearty portions of traditional German dishes, all at quite low prices. Consult the *menú del día* and the chef's suggestions.

International

Blau Mari, Moll de la Fusta 1 (tel: 310 1015). Overlooking the old harbour, it is pleasantly modern and specialises in rice and fish dishes prepared in the new, light Mediterranean cooking style. Prices are moderate.

Café de Londres, Londres 103 (tel: 414 1555). A big new restaurant, with mirrors and oil paintings on the walls, serving classical cooking by Antonio Pacheco, one of the city's best-known chefs. The menu makes use of whatever is best from the market, and for both lunch and dinner the *menú del día* is moderately priced and usually good value.

Flash-Flash, La Granada del Penedés 25 (tel: 237 0990). Modern and efficient with an interesting choice of dishes at moderate prices, this is a favourite eatery of the 'beautiful people', especially at night. *Tortillas* or *truites* (omelettes) and salads are the specialities, and there is also a choice of international dishes.

Network, Diagonal 616 (tel: 201 7238). The design is 'neoindustrial' and includes TV monitors at the tables. Dishes include Mexican, French, Italian and some inspired by tropical island food. Prices are fair.

Petit President, Passatge Marimón 20 (tel: 200 6723). Owner Rosalía Sanahuja and manager Juan Bosco believe that people like choice, so they offer a wide one: internationally known dishes and specialities of other Spanish regions as well as their own creations, varying from the most simple to the most sophisticated. Try *bacallà* which is offered in 14 different ways. The service is personal and the ambience is almost homely. Prices are moderate.

Princesa Sofia, Plaça Pìo XII (tel: 330 7110). A hotel restaurant, on Diagonal in the Pedralbes area, included not so much for its international menu, but as a place for a leisurely and moderately priced brunch from 12.00 to 16.00hrs on Sundays. The **Hotel Meliá-Sarria** offers a similar brunch but at a higher price.

Italian
La Perla Nera, Via Laietana 32-4 (tel: 310 5646). An attractive restaurant with lots of flowers and plants in the dining area. The Italian chef ensures that the flavours are authentic and the pastas are just right, with an interesting selection of dishes to choose from. The ambience is friendly and the service is efficient; prices are moderate.

North African
El Cus-Cus, Plaça Cardona 4 (tel: 201 9867). Omar and Maria make sure that customers are well content when they leave their unfussy, inexpensive Algerian restaurant. Cus-cus (or cous-cous) is the speciality.

South American
Los Ponchos, València 196 (tel: 254 0667). A no-fuss, inexpensive place for meats presented in the style of Argentina and Chile.

El Dorado Petit – a little goldmine

SHOPPING

For many of its visitors
Barcelona's main attraction is its
shops, but nobody should come
to the city expecting a bargain
basement. Barcelona is a city of
merchants imbued with *seny*
and much experienced in trade.
When they smell a market for
anything they have or can
produce, up goes the price. The
most interesting shopping and
window shopping is in quality
items of local design and
manufacture, traditional craft
products and work by
up-and-coming artists, all of
which Barcelona has in plenty.

Hours

Most shops open Monday to
Saturday from between 09.00
and 10.00 to between 13.00 and
14.00hrs and then from 16.00 or
17.00 to 20.00 or 20.30hrs (food
and clothes shops tend to stay
open the latest). Department
stores and some of the *galeries*
(malls) do not close for lunch.
Some shops do not open on
Saturday afternoon in high
summer. Drugstores stay open
very long hours or 24 hours.

Shopping Areas

Ciutat Vella

The old town appropriately has
more antiques than elsewhere,
but there are also shops and
galleries offering the latest
fashions, art and other items. La
Rambla does not have much to
offer: the main shopping area is
to the left as you look towards
the sea, between Carrers de
Santa Ana and Ferran and across
to Via Laietana, including the
Barri Gòtic and the street of
Portal de l'Angel. Portaferrissa

is the principal street for fashion
shopping, and there are
intriguing craft shops in the
streets to the right off La
Rambla.

Eixample

Here the emphasis is on art,
antiques, fashion and design.
The prime area is between
Gran Via de les Corts
Catalanes, Carrer de Balmes,
Passeig de Gràcia and
Avinguda Diagonal.

Diagonal and Sant Gervasi

Avinguda Diagonal has a
number of top fashion shops
along the stretch between Plaça
de Joan Carlos I and Plaça de
Francesc Macià. Off this plaça is
the fashionable Avinguda Pau
Casals, leading into smaller
streets with shopping malls
which have in recent years
become the area for wealthy
Barcelonans to do their
shopping. Further along
Diagonal is another enclave for
shoppers, comprising an El
Corte Inglés department store
and the latest Bulevar Rosa
shopping mall.

Specialist Shopping

Antiques

Narrow **Carrer dels Banys Nous**
in the Barri Gòtic has a number
of fascinating antique shops and
there are more throughout the
barri. **Born Subastas**, Plaça
Comercial 2, conducts regular
auctions where you might pick
up a bargain. For old books and
prints look in the musty shops in
the area of the cathedral and
along Carrer de Ferran. Some
70 specialist antique shops
occupy the **Centre d'Anticuaris**,
Passeig de Gràcia 55, and there

are more along **Carrer Consell de Cent**, between Passeig de Gràcia and Carrer de Balmes. **Barbie**, Ganduxer 33, is one of the antique shops which have opened in the new smart shopping area of Plaça Francesc Masià.

Art

The galleries around the area of Passeig de Born are the best for young artists and contemporary work. **Metrònom**, Fusina 9, is the leader among them; **Maeght**, Montcada 25, is part of an international group. Barcelona's oldest gallery is **Sala Parès**, Petritxol 5, and it remains one of the best. More galleries line this street, and do not miss **Sala Artur Ramon** in nearby Carrer Palla. In the Eixample there are many galleries within the prime shopping area but the biggest collection is on Carrer Consell de Cent between Passeig de Gràcia and Carrer de Balmes, where there are respected galleries like **Eude** (278) and **Carles Tache** (290). Near by is

Keeping up with the news in La Rambla

Galeria Joan Prats, Rambla de Catalunya 54, which has a reputation for good shows. Others worth a look include **Arte Unido**, Plaça Gregori Taumaturg 1, and **Tache Editor**, Juan Sebastián Bach 22.

Books, Newspapers, Magazines
Toc's, Consell de Cent 314, is a high-technology, culture and leisure supermarket, well stocked with books, travel guides and maps, newspapers, magazines, paper and paper items, and music in all formats. Kiosks selling newspapers, maps and guides, magazines and books (some very lurid) are plentiful. Those at the top of La Rambla close only on Sunday afternoon and night.

Crafts

The Generalitat runs the **Centre Permanent d'Artesania**, Passeig de Gràcia 55, which displays traditional and contemporary craftwork of Catalunya. It is a good place to visit first just to see what is available. In department stores and small shops around the city you will find craft items from all parts of Spain, but a search through the Ciutat Vella may be more fun and more rewarding: this is where traditional crafts still continue and where the shops are fascinating in themselves. Decorative candles are a local speciality and the best place to look for them has been going since 1761: **Cereria Subirà**, Baixada Liberteria 7 (off Plaça de Sant Jaume). There are other candle shops in the area of the cathedral. Ceramic items, including decorative tiles, are another good buy. Start looking in Plaça Sant Josep Oriol, Carrer Banys Nous, Carrer Call and Carrer de la Boqueria; but keep your eyes open everywhere as there are many places, including neighbourhood houseware shops, selling both rustic cooking ware and finely crafted pieces. Other things to look for include embroidery and lacework, glassware, fans, shawls, espardenyes (canvas rope-soled shoes), gold and silverwork, and papier mâché objects. You will find specialist shops in the streets mentioned above, and in Carrer de Ferran, Carrer de l'Hospital and Carrer del Carme on the other side of La Rambla. There are more traditional craft workshops in streets off Passeig del Born.

Department Stores
Barcelona's four big stores are branches of national chains and are much like those in other countries. El Corte Inglés is considered a bit more upmarket than Galerías Preciados. Both offer facilities of tax-refundable purchases, packing and forwarding:
El Corte Inglés, Plaça de Catalunya 14 (tel: 302 1212), and Diagonal 617–619 (tel: 322 4011). **Galerías Preciados**, Portal de l'Angel 19–21 (tel: 317 0000), and Diagonal 471–3 (tel: 322 3011).

El Corte Inglés, Plaça de Catalunya

Design

Some say that Barcelona equals Milan as a leading centre of contemporary design; others say Barcelona is less of a leader but is successful at keeping abreast with the foremost trends. You can decide for yourself as you wander the streets and look not only at the objects on display but at the design of the shops themselves. (and of restaurants, bars and discos). Your first stop should be **Vinçon**, Passeig de Gràcia 96. This spacious store, which includes an art gallery, has its own design in housewares and a whole gamut of other items. **B D Ediciones de Diseño**, Mallorca 291, has designer furniture including reproductions of Gaudí pieces. **Artespaña**, Rambla de Catalunya 75 and Muntaner 537, is a government-sponsored national chain offering design from traditional to the very latest in furnishings and other items from around Spain. **Inicial G**, Balmes 458, has useful and nonsense items, gadgets and the like, also of the latest design.
D Barcelona, Diagonal 367, has a gallery specialising in conceptual art, and sells a range of designer items and gadgets.

Drugstores

'Drugstore' in this sense means a collection of shops selling more or less useful things, with a place or places to eat.
The Drugstore, Passeig de Gràcia 71. Open 24 hours every day, it has a supermarket and shops selling books, gifts, perfumes, photo supplies and tobacco, plus a restaurant, cafeteria and bar.
VIP'S, Rambla Catalunya 7. Among its 22 shops, open from 09.00 to 01.30hrs (03.00 Friday and Saturday), you can find food, books, toys, gifts, paper products, records and photo supplies. There are also a cafeteria and Italian restaurant.
Drugstore David, Tuset 19-21. Open daily from 09.00 to 05.00hrs, with more than 50 shops, including some that sell clothes. Reasonable prices and good, simple food make the restaurant very popular.

Fashion

Over the past decade Spain's fashion designers have moved centrestage in the competitive international scene. Creations of the most successful designers can be found around the world, but in Barcelona's boutiques you are likely to find a wider choice of them. Look for names like Sybilla, Roser Mercè, Sara Navarro, Purificación Garcia and others mentioned below. You can also choose from the less expensive models of talented designers who have not yet hit the headlines. This is just a selection of top shops and boutiques; for others remember the shopping malls.
For Women
Bebelin's Consell de Cent 298: elegant, classical designs and famous name collections.
Capital A, Passeig de Gràcia 76: leading Spanish designers are featured, including María Cusata, Gonzalo González and Jordi Cuesta. The shoe salon has the latest designs from Robert Clercerie. Local designer **Lola Barcelò** has shops at Balmes

SHOPPING

Reflecting the look on the streets

228, Muntaner 244 and 502 and in Galeries Turò. In the spacious and elegant boutique of **Tema**, Ferran Agull 10, Spanish designers like the Madrileños, Manuel Piña and Jesús del Pozo are well represented.

For Men
Furest, Passeig de Gràcia 12, Diagonal 468 and Pau Casals 3, has been a favourite outfitter of the city's more sedate gentlemen for a long time. It stocks leading names from Europe and North America. **Jose Tomas**, Mallorca 242, is a young designer who has been inspired by Giorgio Armani. A selection of own label and leading names (nothing much in the vanguard) is stocked by **Leoni**, Portaferrissa 13, València 26, Diagonal 506 and 604, and Casp 99. Although the name sounds Italian, **Massimo Dutti**, Passeig de Gràcia 13, Rambla Catalunya 60, Via Augusta 33 and Diagonal 602, is very much a Spanish success story, based on good design, good quality and reasonable prices with a

growing chain of shops.
For Men and Women
Adolfo Domínguez, Passeig de Gràcia 89 and València 245, is probably the best-known Spanish designer internationally. The two spacious shops of **Farreras**, Passeig de Gràcia 79 and Diagonal 586, have a wide selection of clothing, footwear and accessories for both sexes and all ages. **Groc**, Rambla de Catalunya 100 and Muntaner 385, sells the creations of the fashion leader Toni Miró. The long-established firm of **Gales**, Passeig de Gràcia 32, Diagonal 490 and 596, and Tuset 1, offers many well-known labels and a selection from staid sophistication to zany youthfulness. Quite similar in style and merchandise is **Santa Eulalia**, Passeig de Gràcia 60 and 93, and Pau Casals 8. Leather fashions and accessories are the speciality of **Loewe**, Passeig de Gràcia 35, Diagonal 570 and Juan Sebastian Bach 8.

Accessories

Intimo Due Pau Claris 113. The speciality is lingerie and underwear, and designer labels include those of Conxa Casas and Nikos. This is the place to buy something special for yourself or someone you know almost as well. **Camper**, València 249, Muntaner 248 and Pau Casals 3, stocks the models of leading shoe designers. **Eleven**, Diagonal 466, is a shop of startling dècor, where you would expect the prices of the designer footwear to be much higher than they are. In **Patricia**, Diagonal 466, Miquel Mesquida presents surprising designs in footwear and other leather accessories.

Gifts and Mementoes

Populart, Montcada 22. Down the street from the Museu Picasso, it sells an interesting variety of posters, cards, designs in paper and papier mâché, and ceramic and wood items, which could be mementoes of your visit to Barcelona or inexpensive gifts. Other places to look are **Raima**, Comtal 27; **Konema**, Consell de Cent 296; **La Factoria**, Consell de Cent 412; and **Dos i Una**, Rosselló 275.

Jewellery

Baguès, Passeig de Gràcia 41, in the Modernist Casa Amatller, is a stylish shop with stylish jewellery. The family firm of **Puig Doria**, Rambla de Catalunya 88 and Diagonal 612, has won international awards for designs and jewellery, which often incorporates unusual materials. The original designs of **Ramón Oriol** are available at Bori i Fontestà 11; and designs ranging from primitive to avant-garde are the speciality of **Enric Mayoral**, Laforja 19.

Malls

Malls are mushrooming across the city. This is a selection.

Galeries Maldà, Portaferrissa 22. With 60 varied shops it is the biggest of three malls on this street in Ciutat Vella.

Bulevar Rosa, Passeig de Gràcia 55. The first of the city's malls opened in 1978. Its 102 shops still offer the most central and convenient one-stop shopping. Another Bulevar Rosa, at Diagonal 39, is opposite Galerías Preciados department store and has 39 shops; the newest one, further out at Diagonal 609-15, has 88 shops and is next to El Corte Inglés department store.

Diagonal Center, Diagonal 584. A mall of some 60 shops near the Plaça Macià and fashionable shopping street of Pau Claris.

Via Wagner, Borì i Fontestà 17. A hundred shops in the smart shopping area of Sant Gervasi.

Galeries Turó, Tenor Viñas 14. In the same area, this smaller mall also has tempting shops.

Markets

Antiques

Plaça del Pi, Thursday 09.00–20.00hrs (except August).

Art

Plaça Sant Josep Oriol, Saturday 11.00–20.30hrs and Sunday 11.00–14.30hrs (except August). Plaça Sagrada Família, Saturday, Sunday and holidays 10.00–15.00hrs. Plaça del Roser, last Sunday of the month, except July and August, 10.00–15.00hrs.

Books, Coins, Stamps
Mercat Sant Antoni, Sunday
10.00–14.00hrs: books and coins.
Plaça Reial, Sunday
10.00–14.00hrs: coins, stamps
and postcards.

Crafts
Turó Parc, first Sunday of the
month, except August and
September, 10.00–15.00hrs:
ceramics, glass, enamels, iron
work and textiles.

Fleamarket
Plaça de les Glòries, Monday,
Wednesday, Friday and
Saturday 08.00–20.00hrs
(19.00hrs in winter): be
prepared to bargain.

Sports
The sports departments of
department stores stock
equipment and clothing from
leading manufacturers. Other
good sports shops are: **Esports
Sanjust**, Canuda 6; **Beristany**,
Passeig de Gràcia 94; and
Sapporo, Calvet 8 (very good
for skiing gear).

Sumptuous style at the Ritz

ACCOMMODATION

During weekdays throughout
the year Barcelona often cannot
satisfy the demand for
accommodation in the medium
to top categories of hotels. In
the summer season places with
lower classification get very
booked. Several new hotels are
being built, most with 4- and
5-star ratings. Unfortunately,
other projects which would
have helped to relieve the city's
shortage of good quality
accommodation have been
scrapped. It is expected there
will be increased demand from
both the business and holiday
traveller sectors and that the
availability of hotel rooms in the
medium to top categories will
continue to be inadequate. If
you are making independent
arrangements for your visit to
Barcelona, it is wise to make a
reservation in advance. Spain's
tourist office in your country can
provide some basic information
about officially classified
accommodation but it will not
make reservations.

From the same source, and from press advertising, you can find out details of companies which offer packages of flights and accommodation in Barcelona. A package is likely to be less costly than making independent arrangements, and it is less troublesome. From spring to autumn even cheaper packages should be available to resorts along the Costa Maresme and the lower part of the Costa Brava to the north of Barcelona, or along the Costa Dorada to the south. From these resorts it is easy to make day excursions to the city by public transport, especially by the coastal train services. Tourist offices in Barcelona, and in the resorts, will provide information about local accommodation but they will not make reservations. Information can also be obtained from the **Gremi d'Hotels de Barcelona**, Via Laietana 47, 08003 Barcelona (tel: (93) 301 6240).

Spain's long-standing criteria for the official classification of accommodation have become less dependable, and different regional authorities have applied different interpretations. There has been a confusing array of establishments besides hotels of 1- to 5-star and *gran lujo* classification, such as *hostales*, *hostal residencias*, *fondas* and *casas de huespedes*. Establishments are now having to adapt to higher standards and simpler classifications being imposed by the Generalitat: all *Hotels* (1- to 5-star) will require a bathroom for each bedroom; in *Pensions* of one star 15 per cent of

bedrooms will have to have a bathroom, and in those with two stars at least 25 per cent of bedrooms will have a bathroom. Many places are undergoing remodelling and refurbishing. Many others, unable to meet the cost or challenge of change, will be closing. It is advisable to confirm all prices before making a commitment and it is acceptable practice to ask to see bedrooms before committing yourself. As a rule you will do better booking on a room only basis. Breakfast in a nearby bar will be cheaper and it is an opportunity to be among local people. And with so many good and interesting eating places in the city you do not want to be committed to taking all your meals in the same place.

Hotels and *Pensions*

A selective listing of hotels and *pensions* in different city districts follows. Of necessity, the old-style classifications have been used.

In the Ciutat Vella
5-star
Ramada Renaissance, La Rambla 111 (tel: 318 6200), 210 rooms, parking. It has recently been renovated to a high international standard and offers the usual comfort and amenities of a top-rated hotel. A favourite place of entertainment stars.

4-star
Rivoli Ramblas La Rambla 128 (tel: 302 6643), 87 rooms. Good design has been applied in creating its gleaming modern interior and it has an excellent situation at the top of La Rambla.

ACCOMMODATION

There is an open air terrace and bar with good views. Considering its comfort, services and location, it is well-priced by international comparison.

3-star

Continental, La Rambla 138 (tel: 301 2570), 32 rooms. This is a friendly, well run *hostal* on two floors of a block at the top of La Rambla. Distinctive blue canopies cover the balconies of its front rooms. Try to get one of them if you do not mind noise and want a grandstand seat above La Rambla. George Orwell may have stayed here when writing *Homage to Catalonia*.

Reding, Gravina 5-7 (tel: 412 1097), 44 rooms, parking. A new member of Occidental Hotels group with functional design. Bedrooms are small but well equipped and comfortable.

Suizo Plaça de l'Angel (tel: 315 4111), 48 rooms, parking. A comfortable and welcoming place, very well situated for lovers of the Barri Gòtic and Carrer Montcada areas. The Jaume I metro station is also at hand.

2-star

España, Sant Pau 9 (tel: 318 1758), 87 rooms. Recently modernised bedrooms offer fair comfort, prices are good, and the location, behind the Gran Teatre del Liceu, is very convenient. Its public rooms have the distinction of elaborate décor by Domènech i Montaner and his Modernist collaborators. Tops for atmosphere.

1-star

Nouvel, Santa Ana 20 (tel: 301 8274), 76 rooms. This old-style hotel on a pedestrian street offers few facilities but reasonable comfort. Rooms vary quite a lot so check them first if possible or ask for the best.

In the Eixample
5-star

Hotel Ritz, Gran Via de les Corts Catalanes 668 (tel: 318 5200), *gran lujo*, 161 rooms. For long Barcelona's top rated and priciest hotel, and the luxury of its offerings is undeniable. If money does not matter much but superb comfort and elegance do, you will enjoy the Ritz and its touch of class. By international comparison its tariffs are not that exorbitant.

4-star

Condes de Barcelona, Passeig de Gràcia 75 (tel: 487 3737), 100 rooms, parking. At about half the price of the Ritz you get most of the same facilities,

Main entrance of the Hotel Gran Via

similar comfort and a more homely elegance within a Modernist building.

Regente, Rambla de Catalunya 76 (tel: 215 2570), 78 rooms. Quite similar to the Condes, here there is a rooftop swimming pool which is an added bonus in the hot months.

3-star

Astoria, Paris 203 (tel: 209 8311), 114 rooms. Very well situated for shopping, eating and nightlife in the Eixample, along Diagonal and Sant Gervasi. Classic hotel, unpretentious but comfortable and efficient with moderate prices.

Gran Via, Gran Via de les Corts Catalanes 642 (tel: 318 1900), 48 rooms. For less than a quarter of the Ritz's prices you can still feel you are staying in a palace. The public rooms have splendid baroque decoration and furnishing. Bedrooms and bathrooms are comfortable and the service is adequate.

1-star

Merisis, Castillejos 340, 30 rooms. This is a new hotel with basic modern comforts which is close to the Sagrada Família and Hospital Sant Pau.

Oliva, Passeig de Gràcia 32, (tel: 317 5087), 16 rooms. Old lifts creak to the fifth floor of the elegant block and this simple, family-run *hostal* where all the bedrooms are different but clean and comfortable. Ask for a room overlooking Passeig de Gràcia.

In Les Corts and Pedralbes
5-star

Meliá Barcelona Sarria, Avinguda Sarria 50 (tel: 410

6060), 310 rooms, parking. Modern high-rise building for an international-style hotel with full and efficient facilities.

Princesa Sofia, Plaça Pius XII (tel: 330 7111), 505 rooms, parking. Similar to the Meliá but bigger and a bit pricier, and it scores for having both covered and outdoor swimming pools.

4-star

Gran Derby, Loreto 28 (tel: 322 2062), 39 apartments, parking. Here you have all the facilities of a good hotel, except restaurant and bar, and the extra space and convenience of well furnished and equipped apartments.

2-star

Prisma, Infanta Carlota 119 (tel: 239 4706), 27 rooms. It does not pretend to be more than a clean and comfortable *hostal* and it is a fair-priced choice, convenient to Plaça Francesc Macià.

In Sarria-Sant-Gervasi
5-star

Suite Hotel Muntaner, Muntaner 505 (tel: 212 8012), *gran lujo*, 69 suites, parking. Modern bedrooms, sitting rooms and bathrooms are stylish, spacious and very comfortable, and all for the price of a bedroom and bathroom only in other hotels of similar rating. There are all the usual facilities and the service is very attentive.

4-star

Balmoral, Via Augusta 5 (tel: 217 8700), 94 rooms, parking. Although its compact bedrooms seem a bit overpriced, this is a full-facility hotel and very conveniently placed just off Avinguda Diagonal.

3-star
Tres Torres, Calatrava 32 (tel: 417 7300, fax: 418 9834). Small and recently modernised, with standard comforts, in a residential area.

2-star
Bonanova Park, Capità Arenas 51 (tel: 204 0900), 60 rooms, parking. There is nothing fancy about this hotel and the bedrooms are compact but it is pleasantly situated in a residential area, near public gardens and a games place for children. For this up-market part of town it is reasonably priced.

NIGHTLIFE

Visiting Barcelona and not sampling its nightlife is like holding a bottle of cava in your hand and not popping the cork. The night scene is sparklingly alive with a variety to suit every taste. Live performances range from appearances by world famous artists in every form of expression to nude cavortings which would have made Caligula blush. Music halls emulate the examples of Paris; dance halls are filled with nostalgia for past decades; flamenco *tablaos* evoke Andalucian emotions. Music bars and discos compete not only with the quality of their music and lighting but in the impact of their striking modern design. It is no false claim by Barcelonans that they have one of the most vibrant night scenes in Europe.

Enjoying the best on offer can make for an expensive night out, but there are many venues besides those mentioned below in which you will find good classical or contemporary cultural presentations, be happily entertained or make your own action and fun. Check in the local press, at tourist offices and on billboards. These sources will also tell you about times and where to get tickets. To save time, and money on taxis (advisable at night), try to arrange your programme within a different city district each night. If you want to enjoy the nightlife at its busiest, go out on Thursday, Friday or Saturday nights, and remember not to start too early: at around 20.30hrs begin a half-hour *paseo*; then choose a cocktail bar or *xampanyeria*; start a leisurely dinner at 22.30hrs; by 01.00hrs music bars are getting busy, and discos are humming at their best from 02.30hrs. The usual starting time for opera, ballet and concerts is 21.00hrs, for theatre 22.00hrs; live performances in bars and discos start between 23.00 and 01.00hrs.

Opera, Concerts, Dance, Theatre
Some important venues are listed below. There are many others, including places where the cultural experience is heightened by the surroundings. Check if anything is on at: the beautiful church of **Santa Maria del Mar** (and other churches), the splendid **Saló de Cent** in the Ajuntament, the evocative **Plaça del Rei**, and the lofty **Drassanes** shipyards. You do not need to know Catalan or Spanish to enjoy the city's rich offerings of concerts,

dance and opera. Theatre presentations are predominantly in Catalan but some of the shows, especially comedy and satire, may make sense for those who do not know the language.

Centre Cultural de la Fundaciò Caixa de Pensions, Passeig de Sant Joan 108. Classical concerts are often given in this splendidly adapted Modernist building. (See **Casa Macaya, What to See**).

Gran Teatre del Liceu, Sant Pau 1 (La Rambla 65). Principal venue for opera and classical ballet during a season from September to July. The international opera stars from Catalunya, Montserrat Caballé and Josep Carreras always get a rapturous reception. (See **What to See**).

Mercat de les Flors, Lleida 59. This converted flower market is now a municipally run venue for theatre and dance, where Barcelona's Contemporary Ballet Company often performs.

Palau de la Música Catalana, Sant Pere Més Alt. Do not miss a performance by the Orquesta Ciutat de Barcelona or one of the other symphony or chamber orchestras, jazz ensembles, choral groups and soloists from home and abroad: the experience of being in Domènech i Montaner's fanciful creation is as enjoyable as the music. (See **What to See**).

Poliorama, La Rambla 115. Another theatre sponsored by the Generalitat, where the respected company of Josep Maria Flotats usually performs.

Teatre Lliure, Montseny 47. A theatre which has a resident company doing contemporary work and its own chamber orchestra. The restaurant is very pleasant and popular.

Teatre Malic, Fussina 3. In the area of El Born, where there is a fair amount of avant-garde activity, this is a venue for 'alternative' theatre.

Teatre Nacional and **Auditori**. These two new venues are major additions to Barcelona's cultural environment.

Teatre Romea-Centre Dramàtic, Hospital 51. The Generalitat runs this centre of the dramatic arts, which offers a varied programme.

Teatres de l'Institut, Sant Pere mès Baix. A venue for theatre and dance, sponsored by the Diputaciò de Barcelona, the province's council.

Shows, Dinner, Dancing
Arnau, Paral-lel 60 (tel: 242 2804). A music hall with good Parisian-style shows, very professionally done.

Plaça d'Espanya bathed in light

NIGHTLIFE

El Molino, Vila i Vila 99 (Paral-lel) (tel: 241 6383). Lots of atmosphere, noise, colour and fun in this old music hall.
El Patio Andaluz, Aribau 242 (tel: 209 3378). A choice of Andalucian specialities on the dinner menu and a good flamenco show.
La Paloma, Tigre 27. Early evening and late night sessions of dancing where extroverts like to show off. It is entertainingly 'kitsch'.
Romeria, Casanova 54. Go along here if you want to learn to dance flowing *sevillanas*, which have become popular throughout Spain.
Scala Barcelona, Passeig de Sant Joan 47 (tel: 232 6363). Dinner from an international menu followed by a big scale international cabaret.

Jazz
Jazz lovers should try to catch a performance by Barcelona's own Tete Montoliu and his Big Band

Palau de la Música Catalana

or the Hemanos Rossy group. The 'Cave of the Dragon', **Cova del Drac,** Tuset 30, is an intimate place, long regarded as the city's top venue for jazz. Among other places to enjoy good jazz are: **L'Eixample Jazz Club,** Diputació 341, and **Harlem,** Comtessa de Sobradiel 8.

Rock and Pop
Barcelona is included in most European tours by top performers and it has a sizeable population of talented locals and expatriates. The **Palau Sant Jordi** on Montjuïc is a superb new venue for concerts and there are other venues, like the **Palau Municipal d'Esports** and **Plaça de Toros,** where big names may appear. Tickets are usually sold through record shops. Three multi-space discos which often have very good live music, including that of top international names, are: **Zeleste,** Almogàvers 122, **Studio 54,** Paral-lel 64, and **KGB,** Alegre de Dalt 55.

Cafés, Bars, Discos
With so much on offer, fat books could be written on the subject and they would have to be updated regularly as new places open, others close and what is in fashion loses its appeal for the trendsetters. The places selected here have shown staying power and should survive the vagaries of fashion. They offer anything from drinks before dinner (see **Food and Drink**) through to early morning disco. Some bars and discos have doormen with unfathomable criteria. The only advice is to dress 'smartly casual' and to look trendy. Some

places charge an entry which includes one drink; in others you pay an entry and pay for all drinks. Prices can vary according to the night of the week or depending on whether there is some special event.

Before Dinner

Xampanyerias serve a good choice of cavas by the glass or bottle as well as cocktails based on cava. **Art Cava Fussina**, Fussina 6, in the avant-garde area of El Born, is also an art gallery and is popular with a young crowd. **La Cava del Palau**, Verdaguer i Callìs 10, is convenient to the Palau de la Música Catalana and usually has a pianist tinkling the keys for a mixed crowd of music lovers. **El Cava de Provença**, Provença 236, is a good choice among a few similar places in the Eixample and attracts older, middle-class regulars.

Along **Passeig del Born** are a number of cocktail bars, some with an exotic ambience and unusual drinks. On warm evenings, the bars and their terraces along the **Moll de la Fusta**, overlooking the old harbour, are an attractive alternative. In **Boadas**, Tallers 1 (La Rambla), tiny and usually packed, the owner and her staff are expert cocktail mixers and the cocktail of the day is a good one to choose.

Café de las Artes, València 234, is a fashionable place in the Eixample, where the drinks are relatively inexpensive. In the Sant Gervasi area, **Marcel**, Sauguès 45, and **Gimlet**, Santaló 46, are popular haunts for a young, modern crowd.

After Dinner

Metropol, Passatge Domingo 8, a pioneer of the modern Barcelona night scene, is still one of the essential stops, especially if you like listening to black music. **Nick Havanna**, Rosselló 208, is another music bar which you should not miss, with its sensational design, hi-tech music, lighting and videos. **Zsa-Zsa**, Rosselló 156, has an elegant, calm decor with original touches, and attracts yuppies and hardworked business people in search of a revival.

Universal, Carrer de Maria Cubí, 182–4. Uptown in Sant Gervasi, this is another music hotspot with exceptional decor.

Scape, Aribau 163, is a recent arrival on this street, which has become a focal point of the city's 'in' nightscene. It functions as a disco bar and cocktail bar in separate areas.

Satanassa, Aribau 27. A disco bar with a naughty, sexually ambivalent ambience, which often stages special nights on outrageous themes.

Centro Ciudad, Consell de Cent 294. Here you can play billiards, sit and talk, see art exhibitions and occasional live shows, listen to good music or dance.

Distrito Distinto, corner of Meridian and Aragó. A bastion of post-modernism and a haunt of the beautiful people, it is basically a disco but has live music on occasions.

Poble Espanyol

Choose well among the many places packed into this compact area and you can conveniently have a most memorable night.

This is a suggestion for a night's progress from around 21.00hrs:
La Cerveria — beers from around the world, tasty tapas.
La Cava del Poble — a good choice of cavas.
Tablao del Carmen (tel: 325 6895) — well-rated flamenco.
Denominaciò d'Origen (tel: 325 1797) — for dinner, with dishes and wines from Spain's regions.
Las Torres de Avila — a spectacular multi-space nocturnal venue (now a must on the nightscene).
La Disco del Poble — to dance away the remaining hours.

Sex and Shows

Locals loyal to Barcelona may be reticent about its upfront position in the league of cities where sex is big business. Parading prostitutes are prominent: females and transvestites around the lower stretches of La Rambla, and elsewhere; males along Passeig de Gràcia. Quality newspapers have columns of small advertisements, and there are saunas and clubs where anything is possible at a price.

Some better-known places where sex is the theme are:
Bagdad, Nou de la Rambla 103 (Paral-lel), has a no-holds-barred show which leaves nothing to the imagination. At **Coco**, Balmes 51, young men do striptease to an appreciative audience of single women or couples. In **Martins**, Passeig de Gràcia 130, an essential stop on the gay prowl, the mix of customers is the show: at the bar, on the dance floor and in the back room.

WEATHER AND WHEN TO GO

Summers are hot and humid. The average temperature through June to September is 23.5 degrees Centigrade (74 degrees Fahrenheit) with a peak average just over 25 degrees Centigrade (77 degrees Fahrenheit) in July. Winters are relatively mild with a mix of bright days and others which are overcast or rainy. January is usually the coldest month, with an average temperature around 9 degrees Centigrade (48 degrees Fahrenheit). The most perfect weather is usually during May and October. Pack clothes appropriate for the season bearing in mind that the dress order is to look casually smart and comfortable. In winter and spring take a light overcoat and an umbrella. The climate makes Barcelona an all-year destination. Its attractions function throughout the year too, so when you go

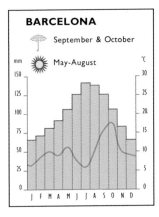

BARCELONA

September & October

May-August

depends on when you are free and what your special interests are. Whatever the season, there is a packed programme of cultural events and entertainment. During August, when Barcelonans leave for the coast or the hills, some restaurants and other businesses may be closed.

Museu d'Art de Catalunya, Montjuïc

HOW TO BE A LOCAL

You need to be around for a long time and to try very hard to become integrated as a local. Firstly you have to decide if you are aiming for acceptance within the Catalan-speaking mainstream of Barcelona society, by the Spanish-speaking sector or by one of the foreign communities, among which the French are the strongest. In this commercially minded city your economic status is an important factor. If you are wealthy your acceptance will be faster, or immediate if you are a multi-millionaire. But if you show some real creative talent, you can be poor and still gain ready acceptance.

It is likely to block your progress if you are negative about speaking any language except your own, although this may be regarded as appealingly eccentric by some. To get in with the fastest-moving stream of Barcelona society it is essential to be conversant in Catalan. If you are really sycophantic there are ways to ingratiate yourself with every group: to Catalans say you admire their *seny* and separate culture, that you prefer Barcelona to Madrid, that people from Andalucia and Murcia are lazy; to those people and other immigrants from different parts of Spain say Catalans are tight fisted and sour faced and say how much you like whatever region they come from; to the foreigners proclaim the apparent shortcomings of both Catalans

La Seu towers over the Barri Gòtic

and other Spaniards, praise their home country and say that Barcelona is the most cultured and progressive city in Spain because it has adopted so much from other countries. The last comment is especially pleasing to the French. The English like to be told Barcelona grew rich because it followed the example of England's textile industry and made itself the Manchester of the Mediterranean.

If you are staying for a long time you will have to decide where you stand politically. Conservatives can choose from one of the parties which espouses Catalan nationalism or the centralist Partido Popular; for those on the left, politics range from deep red to the pale pink of the PSC, which gets the bulk of its support from immigrants to Catalunya and is affiliated to Spain's central Socialist party. Short-term visitors will probably not involve themselves with these things, and are advised to stay out of talking about local politics.

It is far better to talk about football (soccer) and show interest in 'Barça', as Barcelona Football Club is known, commiserating if the legendary club's performances have not been good. The club uniquely unites all sectors of society in expressing loyal support, and its poor fortunes on the field in recent years have caused a common depression. A win, especially over Real Madrid, fills the streets with ecstatic revellers. Going to see a match at Camp Nou, Europe's largest stadium, could be a priority in starting to follow local customs.

You will probably not do anywhere near as well making bullfighting a subject of conversation. The ritual does not have much support in Barcelona and the weekly *corridas* during the summer attract mainly tourists from abroad and other parts of Spain. Participating in another weekly event, if you are a quick learner of intricate footwork, gives you a chance to immediately feel like one of the locals, even to hold hands with them. Every Sunday around 12.00hrs in front of the cathedral and 19.00hrs (18.30 in winter) in Plaça Sant Jaume, circles form to dance the sedate *sardana* which for many symbolises Catalan unity. It is dull to watch but satisfying to participate in.

Eleven musicians, called *la cobla*, provide accompaniment on wind instruments and a double bass.

Two subjects of conversation you are most likely to come across are the traffic congestion and difficulties about housing. The opinions you hear will depend on what stratum of society the speaker comes from. If he or she is living in a luxurious apartment a few minutes walk away from work and is in some way directly benefiting from the city's redevelopment, there will be little complaint. But there will be another view from the person living in some dull 1950s block in an outlying suburb, who has a long journey to work each day and feels marginalised.

Where there is common ground among Barcelonans is the taking of leisure in the city's open spaces — its ramblas, plaças and parcs. As in all Mediterranean cities, it is outdoors that people seek their simplest pleasure, to see their neighbours and to be seen. Stroll down La Rambla any evening or go to one of the many delightful parks in the warm months, and the people of Barcelona will be on parade. Last but not least, forget about the time schedule you keep at home. Follow the local one, especially in respect of eating times and nightlife, or else you will find yourself in empty places without the atmosphere which the local people lend them. (See the **Food and Drink** and **Nightlife** sections). Do not get irritated because many places of interest and businesses are closed during the siesta, when the locals take a long respite from the day's work. Be wise and use the time to rest from sightseeing. You will be pleased you did so if you are later discovering Barcelona by night.

CHILDREN

It seems to be within the character of Mediterranean people to be very tolerant towards children, and Barcelona is no exception — it is hospitable to the young. The city offers a lot for them: plenty of museums and exhibitions; chances to participate in sports and other activities; entertainment and other fun. It is a city which cares about children as its adult citizens of the future, but it is not always easy for visiting children to gain access to all that is on offer. Municipal tourist offices provide information on current programmes for young people arranged by the city council. The tourist offices can also refer you to other organisations which have changing activities and special events for young people.

Theatre and Music

The **Fundaciò Miró** runs a programme of children's theatre (except for the four months from June to September). A weekend venue for children's theatre is the **Jove Teatre Regina**, Sèneca 22. There are also neighbourhood theatre presentations, puppet shows and musical performances by and for young people in a variety of venues, indoors and in the open air, as well as clowns and other entertaining street performers.

CHILDREN

Museums

The city's museums, such as the Museu Picasso, are often thronged with groups of children, who are sometimes permitted to be quite noisy. This can be irritating for others wanting to take a serious interest in the exhibits. If you see a party of youngsters entering a museum or exhibition, think twice before going in yourself — it may be wise to leave your visit for another time.

Many parents will know that dragging a bored child around a museum can be an exasperating experience, but there is one museum which children are likely to enjoy very much:

Museu de la Ciància, Teodor Roviralta 55. It is extremely well planned to give an insight into various sciences and to stimulate an interest in them, especially by children (of different age groups). There are also good periodic exhibitions. *Open*: Tuesday to Sunday 10.00–20.00hrs. *Metro*: Avinguda Tibidabo.

Another museum which is an option for children (of less interest to adults) is:

Museu de Cera, Passatge de la Blanca (off La Rambla). It does not rate too highly by the standards of wax museums but has enough to be fun for children. *Open*: Monday to Friday 11.00–13.30 and 16.30–19.30hrs, Saturday and Sunday 11.00–20.00hrs. *Metro*: Drassanes, Liceu.

For children who are soccer enthusiasts there is:

Museu del FC Barcelona, Aristides Maillol s/n. In addition to various exhibits there are audiovisual presentations on the history of the club, and a view of the stadium from the presidential box. *Open*: daily except summer Sundays and winter Mondays. *Metro*: Collblanc.

Rides
Bus Turìstic

This bus (number 100) operates from 23 June to 16 September and does a circuit around the city, with 15 stops at key points of interest. (See introduction to **What to See** section.) Taking the whole journey, without necessarily alighting at any of the stops, is a convenient, low-cost and untiring way of allowing children to see much of the city. The ticket also applies to use of the Tramvia Blau (tram), the Tibidabo Funicular, and the Montjuïc funicular and cable car; and it allows you to claim discounts at La Muntanya Màgica, Las Golondrinas, the Zoo and Poble Espanyol.

Las Golondrinas

These are small boats which make trips in the old harbour, starting from the foot of the Columbus monument. Nothing much happens but you get a smell of sea air and a different view of the Barcelona seafront. They leave every 30 minutes, summer 10.00–20.00hrs, winter 10.30–13.00 and 15.00–17.00hrs. *Metro*: Drassanes.

Cable Cars

Since 1929 taking a cable car ride high across the harbour has been a favourite outing for children. The towers look a bit ancient, but do not be put off. The service runs between Barceloneta and the Miramar point on Montjuïc, with an intermediate tower (an optional stop or alighting point) on Barcelona Moll (quay). The hours of operation are rather variable so it is wise to enquire from a tourist office when you are in the city.

If you want to combine a funicular ride with a cable car trip, take the funicular from the lower base near the Paral-lel metro station, and then a cable car across the Parc d'Atraccions de Montjuïc to Montjuïc castle, where the military museum may be of interest to some children.

Amusement Parks

The **Parc d'Atraccions de Montjuïc** is a family fun park but perhaps more appealing to adults. There are some 40 machines of various sorts, and a small open-air theatre where entertainments are offered in summer. From late June to early September it is open every day except Mondays. During the rest of the year it is open on week-ends and holidays, but check exact hours with a tourist office. **La Muntanya Màgica** is the amusement park on Tibidabo, the high point of the Collserola range of hills. It has recently been renovated and is a well-run place for all the family. Getting there is something children will enjoy too. Take the metro to Avinguda Tibidabo station and then the old (but not rickety) Tramvia Blau (tram) to the lower station of a funicular which creaks gently up to the summit. Times of services relate to the opening hours of the amusement park, so check locally. There are different types of tickets depending on what you want to do in the amusement park, how much time you want to spend there, your age and the like, so be sure that you get the ticket that

Screaming fun, La Muntanya Màgica

suits you. The most essential experience is to take a ride on the Avion Tibiar — it gives a whirring thrill to any child (and great views of Barcelona). The Museu d'Automatas with its human and animal robots, games and models will also delight some children.

A **zoo** is not really an amusement park but Barcelona's caters well for children. Besides its star attraction of Floc de Neu (Snowflake), the albino gorilla, and other animals, there are performances by dolphins and parrots. It also has a section where children can touch farm animals and pets. (See also **What to See**.)

Poble Espanyol

For children this can be a fascinating place to visit and see the variety of architecture from all over Spain. There are also periodic entertainments for them, presented in the main square. (See also **What to See**.)

Spain in a nutshell at Poble Espanyol

Activities

A very gentle activity is rowing a boat on the small lake in the Parc de la Ciutadella throughout the year, or during the winter in Parc de la Creueta del Coll. From June to September the lake of Parc de la Creueta del Coll becomes a favourite swimming place for children. Then there are the beaches, with a big choice north and south of the city. One of the better ones near the city centre is Mar-bella beach in the district of Poble Nou.

Children enjoy the cycling and scenery on Montjuïc, but they should exercise care as the area is used by motoring schools to put pupils through their paces. Bicisport (tel: 214 4046), located near the Palau Nacional, rents cycles.

TIGHT BUDGET

Investigate what budget holiday packages to Barcelona are available from your country: these often work out far cheaper

than arranging travel and accommodation yourself. If you are looking for low-cost accommodation on the spot, the best area for budget pensions is within the Ciutat Vella, but avoid the part on the seaward side of Carrer Ferran and Carrer de l'Hospital. The district of Gràcia also has budget accommodation and is conveniently situated for exploring the city without too much expenditure on transport. There are budget pensions in the Eixample, best in the area of Sants station and the Sagrada Família. You can stay cheaply in other parts of the city but there will be more trudging around finding a place you like and inspecting the rooms on offer. Camping is a possible alternative.

You will find the biggest concentration of budget eating places in the Ciutat Vella. Look along Carrers dels Tallers, Sitges, Santa Anna and Comtal, on either side of the top end of La Rambla.

- All over the city there are unassuming bars or *sesones* with low cost food and drink. Gràcia is a good area to look.
- Avoid places which display an array of credit card signs.
- Ordering a choice of tapas or raciones (larger portions) can work out more costly than taking the *menú del día*.
- Beer is cheaper if you ask for *una caña* (draught), and a *vino de la case* (house wine) will be the lowest priced.
- Buy food and drink in a market or shop to make up a meal which you can enjoy outdoors in one of the city's many delightful open spaces.

- A small supply of food and drink in your room is a saving standby, but avoid turning your room into a kitchen.
- Walking is not only the cheapest way of getting around the city, it is also the best way to get to know it. Cost saving options for public transport are mentioned in the **Directory**.
- For entertainment, taking an evening *passeig* (stroll) and indulging in people-watching is the cheapest option.
- If you want to sit at a fashionable open-air café, make the most of the cost by lingering over your drink (the locals do).
- Instead of La Rambla, go to the less expensive Avinguda de Mistral, south of Plaça d'Espanya. It has a lively atmosphere in warm weather, with open air bars and a younger crowd.
- For details of free entertainment, consult the local press, look at billboards, enquire at tourist offices and ask the Cultural Information Centre at La Rambla 99.
- For budget shopping, avoid the high class districts. Go into the other residential areas such as Gràcia, and visit the markets.

SPECIAL EVENTS

As well as the events below, each of the city's barris has its own annual celebrations in honour of its patron saint.

January
On the 6th the Three Kings, **Reis Mags**, arrive by boat. Seated on grand floats they progress through the city, showering the crowds with sweets.

SPECIAL EVENTS

February/March

Carnival closes on Ash Wednesday with the symbolic burial of a sardine. Preceding days are merry, colourful and hectic. Celebrations in Sitges are the most spectacular and uninhibited.

April

Sant Jordi, Catalunya's patron saint, has his day on the 23rd. It is also the day when couples express their love by gifts of a book to the man and a rose to the woman.

On and just before **El Dia de la Palma** (Palm Sunday) huge markets sell decorative palms. **Festival of Old Music** (through May).

The Fundació Miró and Nick Havanna are main venues for the **Festival of Contemporary Music** (through May and June). Sitges hosts an **International Theatre Festival** towards the end of the month.

Museu Maricel, Sitges

May

Stalls selling herbs, honey and crystallised fruits are set up in Carrer de l'Hospital (off La Rambla) for the **Fira de Sant Ponç**, whose day is on the 11th. **Maig Coral**, a season of choir music, through June.

June

The **summer solstice** is celebrated with bonfires, fireworks and an abundance of merrymaking. **Sant Joan's day** on the 24th, a public holiday, gives time to recover. The **Grec Festival** starts this month and runs through to early August, with music, dance and theatre, which is of a high standard and noted internationally.

Barcelona's **International Film Festival** starts towards the end of the month and runs for two weeks.

Flamenco Festival during the last two weeks.

September

Diada de Catalunya, the Catalan national day on the 11th, marks not a victory but the taking of the city by Felipe V in 1714. Political manifestations are the order of the day.

Setmana Gran is the week leading up to the 24th – the day of La Mercè, the city's patron saint, who is favoured with its principal fiesta. A special programme of theatre and concerts is arranged. Parades feature *gegants* (giants) and *caps grossos* (big heads); *castellers* build their human towers in Plaça Sant Jaume; the *sardana*, Catalunya's staid national dance, is danced to the strains of the *cobla* band wherever there is space; and the wine and cava flow freely. The **opera and ballet season** of the Gran Teatre del Liceu starts this month (through to July).

October
International Jazz Festival during the last week (through November).

November
International Festival of Fantasy Film in Sitges.

December
The **Fira Santa Llucia** starts on the 13th, the saint's feast day, when the plaça in front of the cathedral and the alleys around it are filled with bright stalls selling Christmas gifts (many craft items), decorations and nativity scenes.

SPORT

In its sports amenities and the quality of its venues Barcelona now rates among the best-provided cities in the world. The main spectator sports are soccer, basketball, athletics, cycling, swimming and tennis. To find out what is on during your stay, look in newspapers or the specialist daily, *El Mundo Deportivo*. Information is also available from the Sports Division of the Ajuntament, Avinguda del Estadi s/n (tel: 325 4362). Exhibitions on sporting themes are held in the Museu i Centre d'Estudis de l'Esport 'Dr Melcior Colet', Buenos Aires 56–8.
What follows is a selection of places for participant sports which are open to the public:

Sports Complex
Can Caralleu, Esports s/n (tel:

204 6905). A pleasant, well-run complex with covered and uncovered swimming pools, and courts for tennis, volleyball and *fronton* (or *pelota* – a fast-moving ball game of northern Spain). Classes are available. Open: 08.00–23.00 for tennis, but it is advisable to check opening times and availability of the various facilities.

Bowling
Boliche, Diagonal 508 (tel: 237 9098). Open: 18.00–02.00hrs.
Pedralbes Bowling Alley, Avinguda del Doctor Marañón 11 (tel: 333 0352). Offers classes. Open: 10.00–01.30hrs.

Cycling
Over weekends and on holidays, from 10.00 hrs to the early evening, **Bicitram** hire out a choice of bicycles from three depots: Avinguda Marqués d'Argentera 15 (for rides in the Parc de la Ciutadella and seaside area); Carretera Aigües s/n (convenient for exploring the area of the Collserola hills); Aragó 19 (for inner city rides). **Bicisport** offer a similar service (convenient for cycling around Montjuïc) from their depot near the Palau Nacional.

Equestrian
El Ecuestre (The Barcelona Riding School), Ciutat de Balaguer 68 (tel: 417 3039). Excursions around Tibidabo as well as classes for beginners and more advanced riders. It usually operates only at weekends.

Golf
It is necessary to present your membership card of a nationally

SPORT

federated club before you can play. These are the three clubs near Barcelona, listed in order of green fee costs, starting with the highest (and poshest). An indication is given of distance from the city. All have comprehensive facilities including swimming pools. It is advisable to make advance enquiries and bookings by mail or telephone.

El Prat Golf Club, Apartado de Correus 10 (08820), El Prat de Llobregat (tel: 379 0278). Nine miles (15km). Three courses and a venue for international competitions.

Sant Cugat Golf Course, (08190) Sant Cugat del Vallès (tel: 674 3958). 12.5 miles (20km).

Vallromanes Golf Club, Apartado de Correus 43 (08170) Montornès del Vallès (tel: 568 0362). 14 miles (23km).

Skating

FC Barcelona, Avinguda Arístides Maillol s/n (tel: 350 9411). A division of the

Inside Camp Nou soccer stadium

Barcelona Football Club. Classes in skating and ice hockey are available. Enquire locally about opening times.

Squash

Squash Barcelona, Avinguda del Doctor Marañón 17 (tel: 334 0258). It has 15 squash courts and two for racket ball. Coaching is available. Telephone to reserve a court. Open: 08.00–24.00hrs.

Swimming

There are beaches north and south of the city, and a number of pools are open to the public, for example **Club Natació de Catalunya**, Carrer Ramiro de Maeztu s/n (tel: 213 4344). Indoor and outdoor pools. Classes. *Open:* 07.00–14.00hrs.

Tennis

Vall Parc Club, Carretera de Sant Cugat 79 (tel: 212 6789). Also has three squash courts. Prices are higher at night. Telephone to book a court. Open: 08.00–24.00hrs. (See also Can Caralleu, above, where court hire costs are lower.)

DIRECTORY

Contents

Arriving

Entry formalities
You require a valid passport to
enter Spain. Nationals of
European Community countries
and some other countries do not
need a visa for stays of up to 90
days. It is always wise to check
the current situation with a
Spanish tourist office or Spanish
consulate in your country.
Visitors from most countries do
not require any medical
documents.

By air
Iberia, Spain's national airline,
and the airlines of other countries
operate direct connections
between Barcelona and most
European capital cities. Charter
companies operate connections
with a number of European
airports, especially in the
summer. There are also direct
connections with New York,
Tokyo and Rio de Janeiro, and
more intercontinental services
are expected. Other intercontinental flights have to be
made through Madrid.
Connections with Spanish cities
are by Iberia or Aviaco, its

affiliate. Between 07.00 and 23.00
hrs Iberia operates an hourly
shuttle, Puente Aereo, between
Barcelona and Madrid. El Prat
airport is 7.5 miles (12km) south
of the city on the C244 autovia.
Its extensive remodelling has
provided four terminals,
increased flight capacity and
many improved and
comprehensive services. Money
exchange facilities are available
07.00–23.00 hrs. The tourist office
is open Monday to Saturday
09.30–20.00 hrs, and until 15.00
hrs on Sunday. There is a hotel
reservations desk. Porters
charge by the number of bags.
A train service connects with
Sants station every 30 minutes
between 06.30 and 23.00 hrs, with
a journey time of 16 minutes.

By bus
There are regular bus services
from a number of countries
connecting with the Spanish
operators Iberbus, Vía Eurolines
and Julià. The new central bus
station on the site of the old
Estació del Nord has good
amenities. Nearest metro station
is Glòries.

DIRECTORY

By car

Barcelona is 92 miles (150km) south of La Jonquera, the frontier point with France, along the autopista A7/A17 (E4). Motorway access from the rest of Spain is along autopista A2/A7 (E4). There can be lengthy tailbacks into the city at daily peak times from around 08.00 to 11.00 and 18.30 to 21.00 hrs, and horrific ones in the late afternoon during the summer on Sundays and public holidays.

By rail

Estació Barcelona Central Sants is the principal station for international and other long distance services. Money exchange facilities are available 08.00–22.00hrs. The tourist office is open daily 08.00–20.00hrs. Access to left luggage lockers is available 07.00–23.00hrs. There is a hotel reservations desk. Porters charge by the number

Beaches are in easy reach

of bags. Many services terminating and starting at Central Sants also stop at the more centrally located Estació Passeig de Gràcia. After improvements, Estació Barcelona Terme-França, near Barceloneta, will be a modern international terminal as well as a station for suburban and local trains.

By sea

Trasmediterránea run regular passenger and car ferry connections with the Balearic Islands and there is a weekly connection with Livorno (Italy) by Alimar. Barcelona is also a port of call for cruise liners. Modern, full-service terminals are part of the project for the old port's redevelopment.

Camping

Within about ten miles (16km) of Barcelona there are 12 camp sites with a capacity of over 10,000 places. They are mostly to the south, off the C246 road past the airport towards Castelldefels. Information is available from Spanish tourist offices overseas. The Generalitat publishes a *Catalunya Camping* brochure annually. The Barcelona Association of Camp Sites is at Via Laietana 59 (tel: 317 4416).

Chemist See Pharmacies

Consulates

Many countries already represented in Barcelona are strengthening their consular presence and other countries are opening new consulates. Latest listings will be available from tourist offices and the police.

Canada, Via Augusta 125 (tel: 209 0634)
Republic of Ireland, Gran Via Carles III 94 (tel: 330 9652)
United Kingdom, Avinguda Diagonal 477 (tel: 322 2151)
United States of America, Via Laietana 33 (tel: 319 9550)

Crime

Snatching of handbags and cameras, picking of pockets, running off with unattended luggage or bags and breaking into cars are the principal crimes against visitors. Muggings to steal jewellery and cash may happen in the seedier areas. At night, especially at weekends and in outlying districts, bands of hooligans sometimes threaten and rob passengers on metro trains and buses. The last part of metro line 1 and bus number 605 are the most notorious. Although the precautions which visitors can take are obvious, here are a few reminders: deposit valuables (travellers cheques, cash, passports, etc) in a safety deposit box wherever you are staying; wear handbags and cameras across your chest and wallets in front trouser pockets; do not be ostentatious with jewellery or cash; keep an eye on your parcels and luggage; do not leave valuables in a car (even a bag holding nothing of value, but left in sight, may be a temptation for a break-in); avoid lonely, seedy and dark areas, use taxis late at night. Do not be alarmed, crime is no worse than in most large cities.

Customs Regulations

Personal effects can usually be taken into Spain without payment of duty. Small amounts of wine, spirits and tobacco (up to 200 cigarettes) are also free of duty. You may have to pay a deposit against duty and taxes on valuable items such as video cassette recorders. For full details of the current allowances and regulations, consult the airline or holiday operator, or the Spanish Tourist Office or Spanish Consulate in your country.

Disabled People

Barcelona shows a good awareness of the needs of disabled people in the provision of special amenities such as ramps, wider doorways and toilets. Special needs should be stated and full enquiries made before making final reservations. Spain's private organisation for disabled people is ECOM, Balmes 311, 08006 Barcelona (tel: 217 3882).

Driving

Breakdown

Detroit, Biscaia 326 (tel: 351 1203) provide a 24-hour towing-in (*grúas*) service and have a workshop. Special arrangements may be provided by an insurance policy bought from your motoring organisation. In the case of rental vehicles, contact the rental company. These organisations have reciprocal arrangements with organisations overseas, and can advise non-members in case of need:
Reial Automobile Club de Catalunya, Santaló 9 (tel: 200 3311); for 24-hour service, telephone 200 0755.
Caravan Club Barcelona, Aragó 416 (tel: 245 0500).

DIRECTORY

Car rental
Some firms have offices at the airport and in the city. This is a selection of firms with their city office addresses and telephone numbers:

Atesa, Balmes 141 (tel: 237 8140)

Avis, Casanova 209 (tel: 209 9533)

Budget, Avinguda Roma 15 (tel: 322 9012)

Europcar, Consell de Cent 363 (tel: 317 5876)

Godfrey Davis, Viladomat 214 (tel: 239 8401)

Hertz, Tuset 10 (tel: 237 3737)

Ital, Travessera Gracia 71 (tel: 201 2199)

Tot Car, Infanta Carlota 92 (tel: 321 3754)

Vanguard, Londres 31 (tel: 239 3880). Also rent motorcycles.

For rental of caravans:
Caravanes Catalanes, Premia 23 (tel: 253 3387).

For rental of four-wheel drive vehicles: Dial, Via Augusta 50 (tel: 238 1250).

Documents
Licences issued by European Community countries are acceptable. People from other countries should have an international driving licence, usually obtainable from the motoring organisation in their country. Spain's Ministry of Transport publishes a small leaflet of advice for drivers. Try to get one at frontier posts or tourist offices. If you are driving to Spain, take advice and get information from a motoring organisation in your country before setting off, and buy appropriate insurance. The most notable peculiarity is the requirement for a bail bond, in case of accident. Road signs and rules are generally in line with those of other European countries, with eccentricities which are only comprehensible after exposure to them.

Driving in Barcelona
Barcelonans have a driving 'discipline' which bemuses most visitors and terrifies nervous drivers (and pedestrians). Your time in the city may be more relaxing if you are not using a car (and you can congratulate yourself on not adding to traffic congestion).

Fuel
The fuel sold is normal (92 octane); super (96 octane); gas-oil (diesel); and *sin plomo* (lead-free — happily, increasingly available). Butane gas for cars is available (24 hours) from Gas-Auto, Carrer K, Zona Franca.

Parking
Street parking is limited. Spaces are indicated by blue road and kerb markings, and tickets are bought from machines on the pavement. Inner city carparks are inexpensive by international standards and they are the best places to leave your car. The building of more carparks is part of the road improvement scheme.

Electricity
220/230 volts AC and 110/120 in some bathrooms and older buildings. Plugs have two round pins.

Emergency Telephone Numbers
Police help for visitors: 301 9060. This is a 24-hour service with interpreters for English, French

and German. The office is at La
Rambla 43 (opposite the lane
into Plaça Reial).
Ambulances: 329 7766 or 329
9701 (Municipal) and 300 2020
(Creu Roja)
Doctors: 212 8585 or 255 5555
Traffic accidents: 092
National Police: 091
Municipal Police: 092
Fire Brigade: 080

Entertainment Information
Daily newspapers (see **Media**),
the weekly *Guia del Ocio* and
the monthly *Vivir en Barcelona*
have comprehensive listings.
Look at billboards and pick up
leaflets and information from
tourist offices and from the
Palau Virreina, La Rambla 99.
The municipal information
service (tel: 010) can also be a
good source of information in
Castilian, Catalan, English and
French.

Entry Formalities see Arriving

Health
Residents of European
Community countries are
entitled to reciprocal treatment
from the Spanish health service
if they obtain form E110, E111 or
E112 from their national health
service. But the best advice for
all foreign visitors to Spain is to
buy a travel insurance policy
from a reputable company
which provides comprehensive
cover in case of accident and
illness. It is also wise to carry a
photocopy of prescriptions for
any medication which you are
taking.
Problems are most likely to
arise from over-indulgence in
drink and food by people in a
vacation mood and caught up in

Look out for the details in La Rambla

Barcelona's heady nightlife. In
summer, health problems may
be caused by too much sun and
eating mayonnaise or 'sad'
salads and tapas; or they may
be a reaction to unfamiliar
tap water (so stick to
bottled water).

Hospitals
There are a number of private
hospitals and dental clinics to
which you may be
recommended locally, and
three centrally located public
hospitals with departments for
urgencias (emergencies):
Nearest the Ciutat Vella:
Hospital Sant Pau, Carrer
Sant Antoni Maria Claret 167
(tel: 347 3133).
In Esquerra de l'Eixample:
Hospital Clínic, Casanova 143
(tel: 323 1414).
Near the Sagrada Família:
Hospital Creu Roja, Dos de
Maig 301 (tel: 235 9300).

Holidays

Barris have their separate feast days when places close. Besides the variable dates of Easter and Whitsun, the principal holidays are:

Reis Mags (6 January)
Sant Josep (19 March)
Festa del Treball (1 May)
Sant Joan (24 June)
Assumpció (15 August)
Diada (11 September)
La Mercè (24 September)
Hispanitat (12 October)
Tot Sants (1 November)
Dia de la Constitució
(6 December)
Immaculada Concepció
(8 December)
Nadal (25 December)
Sant Esteve (26 December)

Lost Property

Go to the Lost Property Office: Servei De Troballers, Ajuntament, Plaça de Sant Jaume (tel: 301 3923). *Open*: weekdays 09.30–13.30hrs. Advise your consulate about any loss of personal documents and if necessary contact credit card companies (see **Money Matters**).

Media

Newspapers

Many daily newspapers from other European countries are available by the afternoon. International editions are on sale in the morning. *El Pais*, Spain's national daily with the widest respect internationally, publishes a Barcelona edition and, on Fridays, a good 'what's on' guide. *La Vanguardia* is the oldest of Barcelona's dailies. *El Periodico*, a new arrival in popular style, concentrates on local news. The two dailies published in Catalan are *Avui* and *Diari de Barcelona*.

Magazines

Spain publishes a huge number of magazines. The weekly *Cambio 16* is a respected news magazine in the *Times/Newsweek* format. For sensationalism and scandal *Hola* is the leader.

Plaça Reial – beautiful but shady

Television

Non-subscription and government-sponsored channels are:
National — *TVE1* (mostly in Castilian), and *TVE2* (mostly in Catalan).
Generalitat and broadcasting in Catalan — *TV3 (popular)*, and *Canal 33* (aimed more specifically at different audiences).
There are also three private stations, and a host of satellite programmes can be obtained.

Radio

Among the many stations *Cadena SER* on MW 828 kHz is the most popular, with easy-listening music and local news.

Money Matters

Banks

Barcelona abounds with banks, local and foreign. Savings banks, mostly also offering exchange facilities, are called *caixas* in Catalan. *Open*: Monday to Friday 08.30–14.00hrs (some banks in the central city to 16.30), Saturday (except June to September) 08.30–13.00hrs. Money exchange facilities are available outside these hours at the airport, Sants railway station and the Caixa de Pensions, La Rambla 30. Cashpoints issuing money around the clock with use of a credit card and PIN are plentiful.

Credit Cards

The major credit, charge and direct debit cards are widely accepted, including American Express (tel: 217 0070); Diners Club (tel: 302 1428); Mastercharge (tel: (91) 315 2512); Visa (tel: 315 2512).

Currency

The peseta is available in the following denominations. Notes — 10,000; 5,000; 2,000; 1,000. Coins — 500; 200; 100; 50; 25; 10; 5; 1.

Tax

IVA, a value-added tax, is currently applied at 6 per cent on most goods and services and at 12 or 33 per cent on luxury items and some services. People resident outside the EC can gain exemption from tax on large individual purchases. Shops will provide information. But think about what tax the goods may incur on importation into your home country.

Opening Times

See **Shopping, Money Matters, Post Office** and **Public Transport**. Businesses work from Monday to Friday, but have varying hours depending on their location, type and the season. In the summer many businesses work *horas intensivas*, 08.00–15.00 hrs. For the rest of the year, general hours are 09.00–14.00 and 16.00–20.00 hrs. Official organisations are generally open to the public from Monday to Friday 08.00–15.00 hrs.

Pharmacies

Known as *farmacias* — as well as selling prescription medicines they will provide free advice about minor injuries or ailments and suggest a non-prescription treatment from their stocks. They are easily identified by a big green cross sign and follow normal shopping hours. During other times they will display a sign indicating the nearest *farmacia de guardia*, which will be open. Local papers also list these.

Places of Worship

The great majority of churches are Catholic. Catholic masses are also said in English, French and German. Other denominations and faiths with communities in the city are: Anglican, Evangelical, Greek Orthodox, Jehovah's Witness, Jewish, Mormon, Muslim and Seventh Day Adventist. Tourist offices and consulates will provide information on places and times of worship.

Police

Officers of the three police organisations all wear blue uniforms and have different, sometimes confusingly overlapping roles.
Guardia Urbana The municipal

Sagrada Família

police are mainly responsible for traffic, and have blue and white checked bands on their vehicles and caps.
Policia Nacional Spain's national police are responsible for law and order and internal security. It is to them that you should report a crime or loss and make a *denuncia* (statement). Their main office at Via Laietana 49 (tel: 302 6325) provides interpreter services. They also operate a mobile office, at the Plaça de Catalunya end of La Rambla or half way down it.
Mossos d'Esquadra Catalunya's police force operates mostly in country areas. Officers protect the Generalitat building.

Post Office

The main *Correus* is at Plaça Antonio López. *Open*: Monday to Friday 09.00–21.00 hrs, Saturday 09.00–14.00 hrs. Other offices: Monday to Saturday 09.00–14.00 hrs. Mail can be sent to you at: Lista de Correus, Plaça Antonio López, 08000 BARCELONA, Catalunya, Spain. Take personal identification when collecting. Post boxes are yellow and some have different sections for different destinations.

Public Transport

On arrival collect the latest *Guia del Transporte Público de Barcelona y su Area Metropolitana* issued by the TMB (Metropolitan Transport Corporation). They have offices at Sants station, Plaça de Catalunya, the Universitat metro station, Ronda Sant Pau 43 and Avinguda Borbó 12. *Open*: 08.00–19.00 hrs. From these offices you can get current information about, and buy, *targetes multiviage i abonaments* (multi-journey and saver tickets). These are also available from metro stations, some buses and *caixas* (savings banks). A telephone information service operates on 336 0000.

Air
Many foreign airlines have offices in the city. The main offices of IBERIA are at Passeig de Gràcia 30 and Diputació 258. For information telephone 301 3993. For domestic reservations call 301 6800; for international reservations call 302 7656.

Bus
There is a comprehensive bus network. One-price tickets are bought from the driver. Most operate from around 05.30–22.30 hrs, and there are a few night services.

Metro
Four underground lines, I, III, IV and V, interconnect with the under- and overground train service run by the Generalitat, which extends beyond the city. Maps of the network are displayed at all stations. For metro journeys there is a single fare regardless of distance. *Open*: Monday to Friday 05.00–23.00 hrs, weekends and holidays 05.00–01.00 hrs.

Taxis
Black and yellow taxis show a green light when available for hire and can be flagged down in the street. Standard rates are shown on the meter and there are supplements for baggage or for trips departing from railway stations and the airport. For information about the 'taxi card'

(a credit card), telephone 336 0000. Telephone numbers of some taxi operators: 330 0804: 358 1111; 212 2222. For chaffeur-driven cars: Limousine Service, Montjamar 24 (tel: 429 1388).

Trains
RENFE is Spain's national railway company. It also operates *rodalies* (suburban trains). Full information can be obtained from travel agents, from RENFE stations (the one at Plaça de Catalunya is central) or by telephoning 322 4142.

Senior Citizens
Ask travel agents about special package holidays in Barcelona for senior citizens from your country. Within the city there are good amenities and many special events for senior citizens, but access for visitors may be limited and fluency in Catalan or Castilian is usually needed to appreciate them fully.

Student and Youth Travel
Barcelona is a good city in which to be young. Regional and municipal authorities, other organisations and young people themselves provide many amenities and there is always a full programme of special events. There are five youth hostels and some 30 'youth houses' (run by young people), as well as cheap bed and breakfast places. Some useful addresses are:
CIAJ, Avinyó 5–7 (tel: 301 1221). *Metro*: Liceu. A youth information and advice centre – the best source of advice for young people.

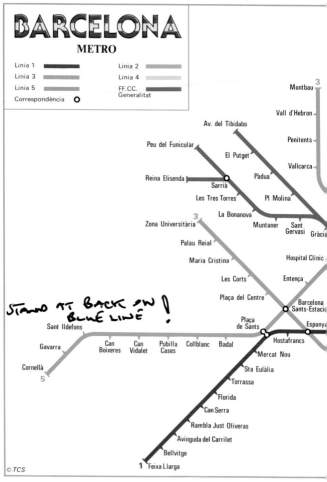

Direcció General de Joventut Generalitat de Catalunya, Viladomat 319 (tel: 322 9061). *Metro*: Hospital Clìnic. Contact for youth cards, which provide discounts at many different places.

TIVE, Gravina 1 (tel: 302 0682). *Metro*: Universitat. Youth travel office, providing student and hostel cards, with details of low-cost travel.

Transforeadors, Ausías March 60 (tel: 245 8362). *Metro*: Arc del Triomf. Youth culture centre.

Telephones

Many hotels provide telephone,

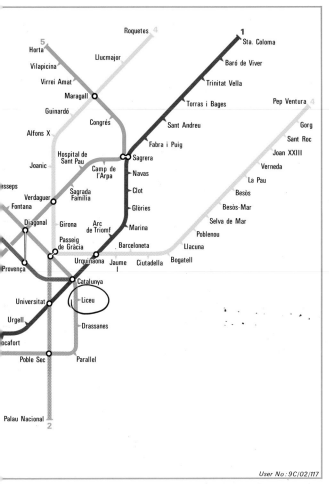

telefax and telegram services, but add quite large supplements. The code for Barcelona (city and province) is 93 and is used for calls from other provinces. To call a Barcelona number from outside Spain dial the international service code applicable in your country, then 34 (Spain), 3 (Barcelona) and the seven-digit number. Public phone booths are plentiful. They take 100, 25 and 5 peseta coins and some accept credit cards. Instructions for use are displayed in a number of languages, as are provincial and international

dialling codes. Many bars also
have telephones for use by
customers. To make direct
international calls put at least
200 pesetas in the groove at the
top (or in the slot of some
telephones), dial 07 and wait for
a changed tone, then dial the
country code, town code
(without the initial 0) and
number. At the Telefonica
locutorio, Fontanella 4 (Plaça de
Catalunya) you can get
assistance, and make reversed
charge calls. You pay after your
call. You can also do this at El
Corte Inglés (see under
Department Stores in the
Shopping section). A cheap rate
applies from 22.00 to 08.00 hrs.
For telephone information, dial
003.
Telefax, telex and telegram
services are available at the
Correus, Plaça Antoni López,
08.00–22.00 hrs and at Ronda
Universitat 23, 09.00–19.00 hrs.
Many businesses also offer
telefax services. For telegrams
by telephone (24-hour service),
telephone 322 2000.

Time
Like most of Europe, Barcelona
is two hours ahead of GMT
(Greenwich Mean Time) in the
summer and one hour ahead in
the winter.

Tipping
Although most hotel and
restaurant bills will include a
service charge, you may still
want to give a tip of between 5
and 10 per cent in restaurants
and for special services in
hotels. At bars leave less than
five per cent from whatever
change you get. The same
applies to taxis. Other people

who usually get tips are carpark
attendants, doormen,
hairdressers, lavatory
attendants, shoeshines and tour
guides.

Toilets
Public lavatories are few and far
between, but there is an
increasing number of lavatory
cabins. There are toilet facilities
at department stores and most
museums and cultural centres.
Bars and restaurants have
facilities for their customers.

Tourist Offices

Overseas
Turespaña, part of Spain's
Ministry of Tourism operates
offices in several countries.
Addresses are liable to change,
so ask locally.
Australia: 203 Castlereagh
Street, Suite 21, Sydney
NSW 2000.
Canada: 102 Bloor Street West,
14th Floor, Toronto.
UK: 57N8, St James Street,
London SW1A 1LD.
US: 665 Fifth Avenue, New York
10022; 8383 Wilshire Bvd, Suite
960, Beverly Hills, California
90211.

In Barcelona
See also under **Arriving** above.
The Generalitat has an office at
Gran Via de les Corts Catalanes
658 (tel: 301 7443). *Open*:
Monday to Friday 09.00–19.00
hrs, Saturday 09.00–14.00 hrs.
In the summer the Ajuntament
operates offices in Plaça Sant
Jaume and the Palau de la
Virreina, La Rambla 99. *Open*:
10.00-20.00 hrs. There are also
helpful, red-coated guides, who
wander La Rambla to assist
visitors.

LANGUAGE

The two principal languages are Castilian (Spanish) and Catalan. This short list of Catalan words and phrases will help you to show courtesy, understand signs, ask directions, do shopping and order services. The person may speak your language, so ask.

do you speak Castilian/English/ French/German? parleu castellà/anglès/francès/ alecany?

yes/no si/no

please speak a little slower si us plau, parleu una mica mes a poc a poc

good morning bon dia

good afternoon bona tarda

good evening bona nit

goodbye adéu-siau

please si us plau

thank you gràcies

my name is . . . en dic . . .

what is your name? com us dieu?

where is. . .? On és . . .?

is it far/near by? es lluny/a prop?

left/right/ahead esquerrel/dret/tot sequit

avenue/boulevard/passage avinguda/passeig/passatge

street/square carrer/plaça

church/monastery/palace/school esglesia/monestir/palau/escola

open/closed oberta/tancat

hour/day/week/month/year hora/ dia (jorn)/setmana/mes/any

Monday to Sunday dilluns, dimarts, dimecres, dijous, divendres, dissabte, diumenge

yesterday/today/tomorrow ahir/ avui/demà

I would like . . . voldria . . .

how much? quant val?

do you have a larger/smaller/ cheaper one/another colour? en tè de mès gran/mès petit/mès bon preu/un altre color?

Numbers

one	un
two	dos
three	tres
four	quatre
five	cinc
six	sis
seven	set
eight	vuit
nine	nou
ten	deu

Local produce displayed with flair

INDEX

INDEX/ACKNOWLEDGEMENTS

The Automobile Association wishes to thank the following photographers and libraries for their assistance in the preparation of this book.

PETER WILSON took all the photographs not listed below (© AA PHOTO LIBRARY).

AA PHOTO LIBRARY 114 Camping.

MARY EVANS PICTURE LIBRARY 16 19th-century Barcelona, 20 Civil War.

NATURE PHOTOGRAPHERS LTD 75 Cistus, 76 Rock Bunting (K J Carlson), 77 Zaragoza (P R Sterry), 78 Ordesa National Park (R O Bush).

SPECTRUM COLOUR LIBRARY 31 Olympic Stadium, 73 Cliffs north of Tossa.